OPENING
THE
BIBLE

OPENING
THE
BIBLE

What It Is,
Where It Came From,
What It Means for You

ROBERT KYSAR

Augsburg
MINNEAPOLIS

Cover image: copyright © 1999 PhotoDisc. Used by permission.
Cover design by Derek Herzog
Book design by Michelle Norstad and Timothy W. Larson

Library of Congress Cataloging-in-Publication Data
Kysar, Robert.
  Opening the Bible: what it is, where it came from, what it means for you / Robert Kysar.
    p. cm.
  Includes bibliographical references.
  ISBN 0-8066-3594-0 (alk. paper)
    1. Bible—Evidences, authority, etc. 2. Bible—Use. I. Title.
BS480.K97 1999
220.1—DC21   99-29449
                                                              CIP

The paper used in this publication meets the minimum requirements of American National Standard for Information Sciences—Permanence of Paper for Printed Library Materials, ANSI Z329.48-1984.

Manufactured in the U.S.A.   AF 9-3594

            3   4   5   6   7   8   9   10

Contents

Introduction ————————————

What's Become of the Bible?

MARIANNE IS A DEVOUT CHRISTIAN who takes her discipleship seriously. She always attends every Bible study offered in her congregation and practices a daily discipline of reading her Bible. Above all, Marianne is honest. She adamantly insists that she understand Christian life and faith to the best of her ability so that she can practice them well.

A few weeks after her congregation called its first female assistant pastor, Marianne came to see the senior pastor. She expressed how excited she was about having a woman clergy on the staff. But then she confessed that she did not know how to reconcile the ordination of women with some biblical passages. She had done her homework and mentioned a number of specific passages that seemed to deny women a place of leadership in the church. "Look at 1 Corinthians 14:34. Paul says, 'Woman should be silent in the churches'! How can we allow Pastor Smith to preach?"

Her senior pastor was impressed by Marianne's honesty and by her desire to understand the practices of her denomination. After a long and open conversation, he suggested that Paul's words in 1 Corinthians 14:34 needed to be understood in the context of the apostle's historical setting. Then he asked Marianne to read 11:4-5 in the same letter. "Any man who prays or prophesies with something on his head disgraces his head, but any woman who prays or prophesies with her head unveiled disgraces her head..." In the process of urging the Corinthians to continue the practice of women keeping their heads covered in worship, Paul clearly acknowledges that women prophesy. In the New Testament, the word *prophesy* means, essentially, what we mean today by the word *preaching*. Moreover, the pastor suggested that 1 Corinthians 11:11-12 assumes the mutual dependence of men and women on one another: "Nevertheless, in the Lord woman is not independent of man or man independent of woman. For just as woman came from man, so man comes through woman; but all things come from God." He then invited Marianne to look at Galatians 3:28. "There is no longer Jew or Greek, there is no longer slave or free, there is no longer male and female; for all of you are one in Christ Jesus."

Marianne made careful notes of each of these passages. But then she looked her pastor in the eye and asked, "Why, then, don't we require women to cover their heads during worship?" And the conversation continued.

What's become of the Bible? To practice its teachings faithfully seems to have become so complicated! There are the writers' historical settings to consider. The relationship of one passage to another must be taken into account. One cannot deny that the Bible sometimes seems to contradict itself. It has been suggested that some things in the Bible are "outdated." How is the ordinary Christian to know and understand all of this? Must we leave the reading and interpretation of the Bible to the experts? If so, why then should the layperson even bother to try to understand the Bible?

Of course, Marianne's question about Paul's teaching concerning women is only one example. There are currently many issues about which sincere Christians disagree and do so on the basis of their reading of Scripture. For decades devout Christians believed that the Bible taught racial segregation. Now there are some who base their stands on abortion, homosexuality, suicide, and many other issues on biblical readings and teachings. Christians seem to agree that the Bible is their guidebook. But with the same guidebook, why do we disagree so much on what it teaches? Is the Bible so obscure in its meaning that you can justify any view on the basis of some portion of Scripture? Some have suggested just that. Is it no longer possible to identify a common biblical basis for life in our world?

These questions invite us to open the Bible and think further about it and its place in the church in the twenty-first century. They lead us to two fundamental questions: What is the authority of the Bible today? How should we read it in the light of its authority? There are no easy answers to this pair of questions. Nor is there a clear path toward some greater consensus among

Christians on the Bible's meaning. But we can, at least, identify these and other questions and discover ways of thinking more clearly about them.

That is the goal of this book. It will not give you a "quick fix" for the problems of reading the Bible and applying its teachings to your life. But it may guide readers through rethinking some of the questions that haunt us today and toward reading the Bible with greater meaning. The chapters of this book address questions that plague many of us who read and study the Bible today.

In each of these chapters, I will try to analyze what is involved in the question before us and supply some information involved in a thoughtful response to it. Sometimes the discussion will describe alternative ways of answering a question. I will not pretend to hide my own views on some matters. But I really want *you* to come to your own conclusions and take responsibility for your own view of the Bible and its interpretation. My role in this process is to clarify the questions and suggest directions for your reflections on them.

You should have your Bible at hand as you read this book. I will refer to many biblical passages as examples of what I mean and, sometimes, as evidence for what I am saying. If you read these passages along with the pages of this book, what I am saying probably will make a good deal more sense to you. Unless otherwise indicated, biblical quotations are from the New Revised Standard Version.

This book is based on the belief that the Bible continues to offer us faith and hope for Christian life in a troubled and changing world. The struggle with what the Bible is and how it might be helpfully read is necessary because I believe, with you, that the Bible is the church's foundation. I invite you to join me in the effort to get down to and understand our foundation.

Chapter One ——————
How Do I Know What Is True?

Every day, national and international news reports seem to pose social, moral, ethical, and spiritual questions for us. Abortion, doctor-assisted suicide, affirmative action programs, immigration laws, sexual morality, family values—the list goes on and on. How do we decide what is right and good in these cases? There are so many differing opinions. How do we know what is true? How do we distinguish truth from falsity?

Imagine that we are investigating a house we hope to purchase. We would, of course, want to examine the foundation of the structure. But, if we were wise enough, we would be curious about what are called the footings of the foundation. They have to do with the depth of the foundation into the earth.

Think of this first chapter as an investigation of the footings of the foundation for an understanding of the Bible. We say that, in some way or another, the Bible informs us of what is true about our lives. But that raises the question of how we know what is true. What sources of truth are there for us?

What Helps Us in the Quest for Truth?

We learn truth in a number of ways. For instance, suppose we want to know if it is true that *Spitfire Grille* is a good motion picture. We have a number of options. We can talk to our friends who have seen the picture. We can read the critics' reviews. And, of course, we can go to see the picture for ourselves. Humans have a variety of resources for determining what is true, especially in religious matters.

Experience
The most common way by which we learn truth is through our own immediate experience. Viewing a motion picture for ourselves provides us a direct way of deciding whether or not it is a

good movie. Experience in this sense has to do with what happens to us when we encounter something. It involves our response to another reality of some sort. Seeing the Grand Canyon for ourselves evokes a response from us that either confirms or denies the claim that it is a magnificent and beautiful site.

Religious people have often discovered truth through personal experience. Luther claimed that he came to the insight of a gracious and merciful God through his experience of studying the Bible. Many of the leaders of the church speak of intimate experiences of God's presence. Jesus and Paul both seem to have had direct and personal experiences that led them to truth. Jesus' transfiguration experience in Mark 9:2-8 confirms his identity as God's son. Acts reports Paul's encounter with Christ on the road to Damascus (Acts 9:1-9)—an experience in which Paul discovers the truth of the Christian faith.

We might say that personal experience is the "common sense" way of learning what is true. On a daily basis through our own experience, we learn whether or not using such and such a shampoo really makes a difference. For some Christians experience figures prominently as a source for truth.

Most often, emotional experiences have helped some to be confident of their faith. Many speak of feeling the presence of God at certain moments in their lives. Others have unique experiences of the activity of the Holy Spirit. But sometimes, too, experience is understood in others ways. Believers have a sense of the truth of their faith that they may speak of as "instinctive." Have you, for instance, ever said, "I just *feel* it's true"? It is the sort of experience that confirms the reality of faith born within the human spirit. Others speak of those moments when they perceived God, Christ, or the Spirit in their relationships with others.

As important as experience is in discovering truth, it is not always so convincing. We read and hear about people having all kinds of personal religious experiences. Some of the reports make us doubt that experience really taught these people truth. For instance, we are rightly suspicious of those who claim to "hear" the voice of God telling them to kill another person. (The story of Abraham's near sacrifice of his son, Isaac, in Genesis

22:1-14 meant, among other things, that God did not desire human sacrifice.)

As a source of religious knowledge, personal experience is suspect for good reasons. Our own personalities shape what we experience. How we have been nurtured and molded in life becomes a kind of internalized filter through which we process stimuli. If I was taught by my parents (both in word and in behavior) that other people are not to be trusted, it is probable that I will tend to experience suspicion about things others tell me. On this level, how I experience life is a reflection of my background.

But personal experience is not always reliable, because it can be too individualistic, too subjective. Each individual has particular experiences. As a society, we challenge some claims to individual experience. We do so in part because we believe the shared experience of a community is more reliable than any individual interpretation of an event. Certainly, there are times when an individual rises up against the community to challenge it, and it is right to do so. Martin Luther King Jr. was a clear example of an individual challenging accepted community beliefs and practices. But in such cases, a community may still form around the prophetic figure—a community that confirms the individual's experience as its own.

Personal experience, furthermore, may not always be reliable because it usually depends on particular moods, conditions, and attitudes at the moment. When we are terribly depressed, we are more likely to experience the whole world in a negative way than when we are in a good mood. Without careful examination and other tests for truth, it is risky to base our lives only on some religious idea that we have personally experienced.

At the same time, personal experience, in large part, is also determined by our culture. Our Orthodox Jewish brothers and sisters, for instance, are puzzled by the notion some people hold that keeping their religious laws is a burden. They experience those regulations not as chores, but as a delight. Our cultural differences are liable to produce very different perceptions. An individual's culture influences what she or he experiences.

Surely, experience plays a vital role in learning religious truth. But any experience needs to be examined. Does the experience introduce me to truth beyond my personality, mood, and culture? As a source of truth, it needs to be supported by other avenues of learning.

Culture

Experience is influenced by culture and so is most of what we claim to know. For the most part, each of us is a product of a particular culture. By culture I mean that larger community of which we are a part. We in the United States are members of the wider North American culture. But within that broader community, each of us participates in smaller groupings—American Indian, African American, European American, Asian American, and so on. Each community shares certain values and perspectives.

A culture is built around certain principles that it claims are true. So, for instance, individual freedom has been a basic principle in the United States and its culture. That principle contains several claims to truth: Humans are capable of being free. It is better to be free than to be subject to dominance by others. All humans are entitled to freedom.

Conscience is a good example of the way we absorb the values embraced by our culture and call them our own. That vague sense of "feeling" that this or that is right or wrong usually reflects the particular cultural setting in which we were raised. What we seem to claim to know, almost instinctively, is pretty much the result of cultural influences on us. As a means of learning truth, conscience must be examined and criticized in the light of our culture and its influence on us.

If culture so strongly determines what we know, we have to ask whether our particular culture is based on and teaches truth. We especially have to ask if the cultural values we embrace are universally true, that is, if they are true for everyone everywhere at all times. There are a good number of clues that the culture of the United States does not have a monopoly on the truth.

One of those clues is the simple fact that cultures change and along with them values change. In the last several decades we have witnessed the decline of many of the values that were once a part of the culture of our nation. Cultural values are not stable. They are constantly changing with nearly every generation.

Compare your life with that of your grandparents. The values that are commonly taught today are, for better or for worse, very different from those of our ancestors. I shudder to think how my mother would respond to an evening of television viewing. She would be shocked by television's lighthearted and open treatment of sexuality and its frequent portrayal of violence.

Cultural values are liable to change. Older values die, and new ones are born. And without permanence cultural values can hardly be claimed as truth for other times and other societies. They offer little in the way of access to truth. A set of values is important for any culture. But they are at best temporary expressions of what is worthwhile and meaningful.

Trying to free ourselves of the views culture has implanted in us is a lot like trying to free ourselves of our skin. The implantation of cultural views is deep within us. They become an integral part of who we are. So, how do we manage to peek beyond our culture in our search for truth? We probably have to say that we never do—at least not entirely.

Still, a number of things enable us to at least imagine truth—and maybe sometimes even to learn truth—beyond cultural definitions. Humans have some capacity to stand up taller than their culture. Those who insightfully critique culture demonstrate that people can rise above their culture to view it critically. Remember, too, those groups of people who, in various cultures, were able to imagine possibilities for themselves beyond their culture. The French Revolution is one example where people did so. The pilgrims' search for freedom to practice their religion in a new land is another example.

But today, we are privileged to have certain means of peering beyond our culture. Thanks to modern communication and travel, we have extraordinary exposure to other cultures. Our own nation is also becoming increasingly multi-cultural. We may live closely with people of cultural backgrounds different from ours. Every day, television and other news media take us inside other cultures. We travel to other parts of the world. As a result, we can easily compare our ways of life with other ways of life. This helps us see the strengths and weaknesses of the society and culture in which we have been raised. It gives us perspective.

Another advantage we have in testing the truthfulness of our cultural values is available. Thanks to the new awareness of ethnic and racial heritage, we are aware that there is no single U.S. culture. Our nation is comprised of people of a variety of backgrounds, not all of which are European or of European descent. Each group has its own cultural practices and virtues. So, on a daily basis we witness the values embraced by sisters and brothers of many cultural backgrounds.

Cultural values are not necessarily truthful in and of themselves. But by evaluating the things we have been taught to treasure as true, we can glimpse the possibility of knowing the truth. Cultural values need to be criticized, assessed, and tested if they are to provide us knowledge of what is true. Needless to say, much that is part of our understanding of religious truth is blended in with the values of our culture. That makes the assessment of cultural values all the more important, but equally all the more difficult. Confusion of religious truth and what a culture claims to be true is dangerous. For instance, are some of our most common understandings of Christian morals really not so much Christian as they are North American? Views of human sexuality in other cultures may be a good example of how Christians interpret morality from a cultural context.

Reason

We need to be critical of the potential of both experience and culture to bring us truth. That critical thought is itself part of another classic source of discerning truth: human reason. Reason involves the capacity to think clearly and to see connections between ideas. It entails rational thought that seeks to understand causes and consequences. Reason employs logic, that is, the ability to see that two truthful statements may mean that a third statement is also true. Most significant about reason is that it draws upon the human capacity to go outside of oneself and view something at a distance and without self-interest, with a degree of objectivity.

In Western cultures, reason has enjoyed a place of prominence, not least of all in science. Scientific method is based on setting out a hypothesis, acquiring evidence (for example, laboratory experiments), and reaching certain conclusions about the hypothesis based on the evidence. But reason has also played a significant role in religion. Both Jesus and Paul employed reason in their teachings. For instance, Jesus argued that, if one was permitted to work on the Sabbath in order to save an animal, then healing a human on the Sabbath did not violate the commandment that it be a day of rest (Matthew 12:9-14). It is a matter of simple logic.

In the history of Christian thought in later centuries, reason was sometimes believed to be the primary source of knowledge. Anselm, a great eleventh-century theologian of the church, spoke of "faith seeking understanding." Reason was the means by which he sought to think through faith in order to come to some clearer intellectual comprehension. With reason, Anselm proposed an argument for the existence of God based on the simple fact that other things existed.

Reason is still a common way of learning religious truth. An example is the argument that the beauty of nature proves there is a God. Or, if one believes that God loves humanity, we cannot then logically claim that God brings disasters and causes human tragedies. Most of us try at least to think logically about our faith. Of course, to do so sometimes brings us up against serious contradictions in our faith. If God determines the course of our lives (what is sometimes called "providence"), what then of our freedom? What is the logical relationship between God's providential care for us and our own decisions?

Most of us recognize that reason is important in our Christian faith and life. We want things to hold together logically around a center. So, we seek an understanding of our faith that is a rational and reasonable whole.

But we may also be acutely aware that faith cannot be supported entirely by rational thought. We recognize that reason has its limits. Some things may be true without being entirely rational. Christ's resurrection from the dead defies normal human reason. But we believe it to be true. Reason also resists the acceptance of what we call "paradox." Paradox is the belief that a truth may be composed of two equally true statements that contradict one another. For instance, we say that it is true that Christians are, at the same time, both saints and sinners. Reason, then, has limits in terms of what it can teach us about truth.

Reason also is limited by the fact that, like the whole of our lives, it is influenced by culture. For the most part, the reasoning many people use is a product of Western European culture. Talk with an elder in an American Indian community, and you may encounter a different kind of human reasoning. But we must also admit that reason is tainted with human sin. Adolf Hitler reasoned with a kind of logic that led him to the conclusion that the Aryans comprised the master race. Consequently, in Hitler's view, Jews and others had to be eliminated.

With all of its limitations, we need reason to help us analyze and understand our experience and our culture. We also need it to seek understanding of our faith, even when our faith need not be entirely reasonable and logical.

Tradition

What is held to be true always stands on the shoulders of the past. Seldom, if ever, do we learn a new truth without the aid of what was learned by our ancestors. That is particularly the case with Christian truth. The earliest Christians were very much aware of their Jewish heritage. We still acknowledge that indebtedness by the presence of the Old Testament in our Bible. Furthermore, what most of us regard as the truths of Christian life and faith are rooted in the church's history. We recognize those roots by using the church's ancient creeds in our worship (for example, the "Apostles' Creed"). We might even go so far as to say Christians simply accept as truth what the church has passed on to us.

But the matter is more complicated than that. Those in the past who discerned and spoke Christian truth were also products of their cultures. Just as we are shaped and molded by our culture, so too were they. What they understood to be true, they saw through the eyes of their time and place. Moreover, when they expressed their insights, they had to do so within the language of their culture and with the ways of thinking it provided.

An example of this is a view of the meaning of Christ's death that arose in the Middle Ages. In that culture, the lords owned the land and livestock. Serfs worked the land and cared for the livestock in return for a subsistence living. If the serfs offended their lord in some way, by accidentally killing a sheep, say, they had to provide him "satisfaction" (for instance, by giving him another sheep). They had to give the lord something that *satisfied* his sense of loss or injury. In that cultural setting and on the basis of some biblical evidence, Christians thought of sin as offending God. Christ's death was then conceived as a "satisfaction" offered to God to make up for the offense of sin. Hence, the truth of the meaning of Christ's death was conceived and expressed in terms of the culture of the time.

We do the same thing today when trying to understand God and Christ. We may think of what Christ has done for us in terms of human relationships. Such relationships are a common theme in our society. We know that in associations with others we sometimes do something that strains the relationship. We might grasp the meaning of Christ in terms of how, in Christ, God offered us divine forgiveness for the sin that has strained or broken our relationship with our Creator. Like our medieval Christian sisters and brothers before us, we use our own cultural setting to understand and express the truth of our faith.

Consequently, Christian tradition is very valuable to us, but we cannot simply repeat it. Rather, the truth we inherit from the past must be rethought and put into new language. Church tradition passes on to us a body of truth that is in another language and springs from other ways of thinking than our own. So the greatest honor we can pay those who have preceded us in the faith is to take their gift and translate it into our own way of speaking. Much the same is true of biblical truth as we will see in future chapters.

But there is another sense in which church tradition, as important as it is, does not suffice. New issues in our contemporary world also require that we do more than simply repeat the truths of the Christian tradition. For instance, the church's views of war in the past are valuable. But the possibilities of nuclear war present us with entirely new issues. In past centuries the church has spoken of "just war": warfare necessary to halt the spread of evil in the world. The two world wars of the twentieth century were cases of what many Christians regarded as wars to preserve justice. But with the likelihood of nuclear disaster, what would constitute a "just war"?

Other issues are just as challenging. The technology of life-support systems forces us to ask questions about the quality of life and not merely value existence at any level of quality. Such technology has resulted in a rethinking of medical ethics. When is a person actually dead? How long should we provide life support to a person?

We need tradition to learn truth. We probe the mysteries of the unknown with the tools our heritage provides us. But tradition alone does not assure us of discovering what is true for us. It only guides us. But out of tradition comes the source of truth about which we are most concerned in this book—the Bible.

The Bible

The Bible is an authority for truth established by the church and passed on to us through tradition. That is to say, the church declared the Bible to be its authority for matters of salvation. It elevated the collection of writings we call the Bible to the status of the basic source of Christian truth. It made that collection of writings its "canon," meaning the standard by which it would judge the relative truth of any religious statement or way of life. The process of canonization took place over a period of time. For the most part, all the church councils and officials did was to acknowledge that congregations were already using these writings as a measuring rod for determining truth and falsehood. In fact, the church created the Bible. There were congregations of Christians before there was a canon of truth by which they lived.

To claim the Bible as authority for Christian faith, therefore, is to accept the ancient church's decision that certain writings provide Christians a source for the most important of life's truths. If we affirm the Bible's authority, we also confess our faith that God led the early church to declare these documents its canon.

One of the first and most important things about biblical authority, then, is that faith in Scripture is a second step of faith. To believe this collection of writings is in some way God's saving message for humanity is derived from a faith in God, in God's work in the church. This doesn't lessen the value of Scripture as a source for truth. It simply acknowledges how our faith in Scripture depends on faith in God—not the other way around.

The next chapter will explore what it is we can expect to learn from the Bible. In what sense is the Bible authority for us? For now we need simply to ponder the fact that the Bible is closely tied to the church, without which there very well might be no Bible. That fact is important in understanding the Bible's authority and how it provides us access to certain truths.

Voices in the Search

We have a number of tools by which we might learn what is true: experience, culture, reason, tradition, and the Bible. Each of these is closely related to the others. So it is not possible to make use of any one tool without the others. This fact is important when considering the Bible as a special means of learning the truth.

A Discussion Circle

Imagine a circle of five chairs. Also imagine that Experience, Culture, Reason, Tradition, and the Bible are persons and each is seated in one of the chairs. You are sitting in the center of the circle on a pivoting chair. Imagine yourself turning your chair to listen to each of the speakers in this discussion.

The Bible speaks first and begins the discussion. The Bible reports the call of Abram found in Genesis 12:1-4. God speaks to Abram in verses 1-3. First, God tells Abram to depart on a journey to a "land" God will show him. Then God makes a series of promises to Abram: He will become a great nation with a great name (verse 2). God will bless him and make him a blessing (verse 2) and will bless those who bless him and curse those who curse him (verse 3). The passage concludes with Abram obediently doing what God had commanded.

Culture responds first: "God isn't very realistic. That's asking a lot of Abram. We don't just get up and move without knowing where we are going or even exactly why! Abram is not wise in leaving his home and family."

Reason chimes in: "I agree with you in part, Culture. God's request is irrational. But notice what Abram has to gain. There are consequences to his obedience: blessing, greatness, and divine protection. Of course, I need to know what exactly the word 'blessing' means in this passage. But it really comes down to this: Can God be trusted? Is the divine promise worthy of Abram's obedience?"

Experience has listened intently and now speaks: "You are absolutely right, Reason! I know you can't always trust what another promises. My life is cluttered with broken promises. But I am glad that Abram can trust what God tells him. It sounds like an exciting adventure; that's for sure!"

Culture: "But it is an irresponsible adventure, don't you see? You can't just up and leave your family! Those connections are important, and Abram has a moral obligation to his relatives."

Reason: "Moral obligations are relative. You must set priorities among them. That's not the issue here. The issue is that Abram acts out of self-interest. He's got a lot to gain by his obedience."

Experience: "Reason, you are too cold and analytical about all of this. You always are. This is scary business! I admire Abram. I bet that if God talked directly to you, you would respond."

Reason: "First, I can't imagine God speaking—at least so we actually hear a voice. The whole story is strange. I think . . ."

Tradition interrupts: "Now wait just a minute! History is filled with those who believed that God called them. You can't just dismiss all those people. Moreover, this is an important story. It begins the whole idea that Jewish and Christian faith is a journey, a pilgrimage. There is a great deal of value in that notion of life."

The Bible speaks again: "Yes, Tradition, you are right on that point. I'll tell you how Abram's journey launched a long pilgrimage, first for the Hebrew people and then later for Christians as well. The Hebrew people . . ."

Experience: "We'll hear your story later, Bible. For now I am interested in what difference this passage makes for my life. Can anyone help me with that?"

The group is silent for a time, each one looking at the others. Finally, Experience takes up its own question: "I suppose that this story has something to do with divine promise and my willingness to trust that promise. But none of you has convinced me that I can trust this promise."

The conversation continues long into the night. You begin to get dizzy from spinning your chair around to face the speakers.

In some such manner as this, reading Scripture evokes responses from all those sources of truth. And as a reader you pivot your chair toward each to hear what it has to say.

Hearing the Voices

The person who is sitting in that central, pivoting chair makes all the difference. To whom you will listen depends on your personal experience and the particular tradition to which you have been exposed. Different Christian traditions (or denominations) tend to emphasize these sources in different ways. In some circles, personal experience sits in the honored position. It is more valuable and is ranked higher than the other sources of authority. Ancient tradition figures prominently in many Christian bodies. For instance, in classic Roman Catholicism the church assumed responsibility for the proper interpretation of Scripture out of its tradition. Anglicanism and the Episcopal Church have most often argued that reason, tradition, and Scripture in combination offer Christians their authority. Lutheranism has tended to emphasize the ancient creeds as summaries of the biblical faith and essential to understanding the truth of the Bible.

Two further observations may prove helpful. First, the Bible occupies only one of the chairs. It is but one source of truth among many of which Christians avail themselves. Scripture is not the sole authority for Christian life, even though some Christians may claim it to be. One may soon see that the other sources of knowledge are always involved in the interpretation of Scripture.

Second, culture is a source of truth that permeates all the others. Experience, reason, tradition, and even the Bible are all conditioned by cultural setting. In that sense, perhaps our imaginary conversation should have Culture lending its voice to those of all the others as they speak! There is no way to escape the fact that truth is packaged in the language and ways of thinking of a particular culture. We need, therefore, in our discussion of the role of the Bible in contemporary life to be sensitive to culture. This sensitivity is an important part of discovering what we can expect of the Bible.

Chapter Two ———————————
What Can We Expect of the Bible?

Expectations often influence experience. We are not surprised, therefore, to learn that the expectations we have of a book affect our reading and understanding it. You read a novel by a particular author and find it engaging and thoughtful. So, you turn next to another novel by the same author, expecting it to be as good as the first. Whether or not the second book disappoints you, your expectations clearly led you to read more written by this person.

Expectations of what the Bible teaches are immense. We hear so many claims for what the Bible contains. Many assert that the Bible tells us all we need to know for a happy and successful life in this world. It will solve all our problems, some argue. The common expression that the Bible is the "word of God" creates all kinds of expectations. Reading the Bible, we anticipate learning all there is to know about God. Even allegations for what great literature the Bible is form hopes for one long literary masterpiece.

All these claims contain an element of truth. But because of such lofty claims, many have been sadly disappointed when they actually started reading the Bible. One young Christian confessed to me that he enthusiastically began the Bible with the hope of reading it cover to cover. But he soon found it utterly boring for the most part and totally irrelevant to his life. Fortunately, he wanted to continue his project but thought it best that he have some guidance in his reading.

Declarations of the value of Scripture have not always been responsible. The claims have resulted in some people feeling the church has betrayed them by the way it represents the Bible. If reading the Bible is influenced by our expectations of it, then we should clarify just what we can expect of the Bible. This isn't to say that that the Bible can never surprise us. It can. Yet I do think that false expectations can dull our reading experience.

This chapter is divided into two main parts in an effort to offer some clarification of what we might realistically expect of the Bible. The first part looks at what the Bible is. The second part examines how the Bible is an authority for us.

What Is the Bible?

To respond to this question requires a series of statements, beginning from the bottom and moving up. That is, let's face the reality of the human nature of the biblical documents before moving to their more lofty qualities.

An Ancient Book from a Number of Cultures

The documents that comprise the Bible originated over a period of nearly three centuries. Consequently, the Bible reflects numerous cultures. Actually, the earliest traditions embedded in the Bible took shape in cultures whose identities are obscure. But clearly the dominant biblical cultures are three. The Hebraic culture involved the society of the Hebrew people from around a thousand years to five hundred years before Christ. The second important culture was that of early Judaism. It dates from the time of the restoration of Jerusalem, after the people returned there from their dispersion (around 500 B.C.E.), through the period of the birth of Christianity. (Out of respect for our Jewish sisters and brothers, I prefer to use the designations "Before the Common Era"—B.C.E., and "The Common Era"—C.E.) The third prominent culture was that of the Roman Empire in the first century of the Common Era. The empire's culture is called "Hellenistic" because of the Greek influence on it. It originated in the fourth century, B.C.E., and affected the culture of early Judaism.

The three languages in which portions of the Bible were written arose from these three dominant cultures. Hebrew is, of course, the language of the Hebrew culture. Some Aramaic also appears in the Old Testament (for example, Daniel 2:4—7:28) and some scattered words in the New Testament (for example, Mark 15:34). It was one of the languages of early Judaism and Jesus' native tongue. The Greek of the New Testament was commonly used throughout the Roman Empire during the first century, C.E.

In every case biblical materials reflect their roots in one of these cultures. So, for instance, we find portions of the Old Testament taking for granted that wives and children constituted the husband's property. The easy divorce procedure described in Deuteronomy 24:1-4 assumes a husband is free to send his wife away at will. The "certificate of divorce" was the woman's means of showing that she had been released from her husband's ownership. The writings arose from particular cultural situations and employ the language and ways of thinking of that culture.

As a cultural product, the Bible also reflects human prejudice. For instance, the word *gentiles* (referring to anyone who is not a Jew) is sometimes used in the New Testament in a pejorative way. (Read, for instance, Matthew 6:7 and 18:17.) That use reflects the Jewish animosity toward gentiles. But prejudice can take other forms as well. Particular New Testament writings often betray an interest in preserving (or maybe reinstating) male dominance. Examples of this tendency are found in the passages that describe proper behavior in the family and in some references to women. (Read, for instance, Ephesians 5:21-33 and 1 Timothy 2:8-15.)

Readers of the Bible should be aware of the simple and obvious fact that it is a product of these cultures. Moreover, the Bible expresses some of the tendencies and prejudices typical of us humans. To expect otherwise is to misunderstand what the Bible is. It is surely more than a product of culture. But as we will see, the interpretation of Scripture needs to be realistic about these human and cultural features.

A Collection of Many Literary Forms

One of the reasons the Bible is often called a literary masterpiece is the fact that it contains so many different literary forms. Within its pages we can find ancient types of history, such as an account of the conquest and settlement of Canaan by the Hebrew people (see Joshua) and the story of the spread of the Christian church (see Acts). But it also contains a vast amount of poetry including, for instance, the book of Psalms and Philippians 2:6-11. Wise sayings are found in the book of Proverbs. The literary form of the four Gospels is a kind of preaching through story. The Bible's literary forms also include prophetic utterances (see Isaiah), epistles (formal or religious letters, such as 1 and 2 Corinthians), and sermons or collections of sermon fragments (perhaps 1 Peter). Yet another form is apocalyptic, as exemplified in Daniel 7–12 and Revelation. This was a special literary form developed in Judaism. The apocalyptic form was used by Jews and the earliest Christians to speak of God's eventual triumph over the forces of evil.

Forms of speech also vary. The prophets, for instance, sometimes speak in strong and condemning language (for instance, Amos) and sometimes in reassuring and comforting ways (for example, Isaiah 40). Jesus uses pithy sayings comparable to the language found in the wisdom literature of the Old Testament. But Jesus also tells simple stories we call parables. Paul sometimes sounds as if he is debating with an imaginary opponent (for example, Romans 6:1-2) and sometimes recites creeds he has received from the church before his time (for instance, 1 Corinthians 15:3-7). Tucked away in what appears to be a kind of history, we are likely to find fable (see Numbers 22:22-30 in which a donkey talks) or analogy (see Judges 9:8-15 in which trees speak).

What should we expect as a result of this variety of literary and language forms? Among other things, we should not expect to read all parts of the Bible in the same way. We know that we read poetry in a different way than we read history. Correspondence has a particular directness and immediate presence of the author that other forms do not have (such as Proverbs). We know that when we are reading a story in which animals and trees talk, we are to treat it differently from a prophetic condemnation of a nation's sin. Readers need to be aware of the literary form of the passage they are reading or else they may misunderstand it (see chapter 5). Expect to be surprised by the Bible's shifts of literary forms and language.

A Collection of Community Documents

The biblical books arose out of specific religious communities and sought to express the faith of those communities. The authors spoke for and to a specific group of believers. The writers' individuality is not nearly as important as the communities for which they wrote. As a matter of fact, the majority of the biblical books tell us next to nothing about their authors. Typical of ancient writings, in many cases the authors are never even named. Tradition has given the four Gospels the names or their authors—Matthew, Mark, Luke, and John. But those books never name their authors internally. Paul is one of the few authors about whom we can gain some knowledge on the basis of what he wrote. This is due, in large part, to the personal form of the epistle. In letter writing, the identity of the author is often important.

Many of the biblical books record the traditions of their communities. They put into written form the stories, the histories, the crises, and the hopes of a people of faith. This means that in many cases what we find in writing in the Bible originated in oral communication. In the first three Gospels, scholars discovered that the story of Jesus was told in short segments that they call "pericopes." The segmentary nature is a result of these separate episodes being passed on by word of mouth for years before they were written down. Like other parts of the Bible, each of the Gospels arose from among a particular group of people and preserved that group's stories.

When we read the Bible, we should anticipate community literature. Expect, therefore, to put aside the modern fascination with knowing the author's identity and personality. Expect to think of each author serving a community.

Reading the Bible can be, perhaps, like reading a weekly small-town newspaper. Such a newspaper is written for a very specific audience. It tries to capture the stories that are uniquely important to the community. Of course, the Bible is not a newspaper, but with small-town weeklies it shares a community base. Individuality, then, is less important than the community.

The psalms are good examples of this feature. They were written to be used in the community's worship services. Even in cases where psalms are written in the first-person singular ("I" and "me"), it is understood that the whole community is included.

A Faith Story

As a whole, the Bible is a single story of faith. It sketches a long journey of faith, beginning with Abraham and his descendants and concluding with the Christians scattered throughout the Roman Empire. It speaks of the origin of faith, of the struggles and crises of faith, of divisions among the people who embraced the same faith, of the life that grew from faith, and of the hopes encompassed in the faith.

If we could read the Bible from cover to cover without knowing anything about the story, we would find between those covers all the features of a great plot. It holds us in suspense at times. For instance, we wonder if the Hebrew people will survive their exile into foreign lands without losing their faith. It surprises us with sudden turns, as when Christ is raised from the dead. It has flashbacks. First and Second Chronicles retell a story we have already read, but do so with peculiar twists and interpretations. Like a good novel, the Bible includes subplots within the larger story line. These stories within stories can be found, for example, in the Gospels' parables of Jesus. Also like a good novel, the Bible has a climax. This climax is in the birth and ministry of Jesus. But the story of Jesus' birth and ministry is told four times with different emphases.

Expect the Bible to tell you an elaborate tale of religious faith. This collection of individual books hangs together around one God who is the central character of the story from its beginning in creation (Genesis 1–3) to its end in a re-creation (Revelation). In God and the faith God evokes in people is lodged what is most important about this book.

In What Sense Is the Bible Authority?

The nature of the Bible as a story of faith points to where we should to look to find its authority for our lives. Answering the questions of the Bible's authority entails answering a slightly different question: What does the Bible's faith story teach us? In trying to nail down a response to this question, we will come to greater clarity regarding the Bible's authority. The Bible's faith story teaches us at least four things.

God Seeks a Relationship with Us

The biblical faith story features God and most especially God's determined effort to enter a relationship with humans. From the beginning of Bible's story, God works to associate with the creatures who exist because of the divine word (Genesis 1). They are made in the image of their Creator (Genesis 1:26-27). This already suggests they are related to God. The rest of the story entails God's approaching humans and soliciting their response.

How can we understand this relationship God seeks? The most we can say, in summary of the Bible story, is that God strives for a loving engagement with humans. We might simplify this relationship by a comparison with friendship. God seeks a friendly and loving relationship with humans. (Read John 15:14-15.) As a friend does, God cares about our welfare and seeks to nurture us in every way. Although we don't want to reduce God to the status of buddy, the friendship analogy does have merit, and it helps us grasp the intimate relationship God desires to have with us.

As mentioned, the Bible's story of faith reaches its climax in the story of Jesus. In particular, the New Testament claims Jesus' death and resurrection create a new possibility for a loving relationship with God. The New Testament documents use a variety of expressions to state how it is Christ's death and resurrection opened new access to God. Many of those expressions are metaphors. The language of these metaphors compares what Christ did with changes in human relationships. Like slaves who have had their freedom purchased and are "redeemed," so we are set free by Christ's death.

In whatever language it is expressed, the point seems to be that God acted in Christ to create a new connection between us and our Creator. Christ's decision to face death is an act of sacrificial love that releases the power of God's love in our lives. God cares so much for humanity that in Christ, God experiences and defeats our most dreaded enemy—death. God shows us that the divine power of life is greater than even death. The Jesus story narrates the extremes to which God goes to make the loving relationship available to us and provides us the opportunity to reestablish our lives bonded with God.

The Bible story, of course, insists over and over again that humans resist a relationship with the Creator. But the central theme of the story is that God relates to humans in love *despite* our stubborn resistance. Human reluctance to accept God's offer never defeats a divine determination to be a loving friend.

The authority of the Bible exists in its central theme. Scripture tells its story of this radical character, God, who will go to any length to win humans over to a relationship of love. Jesus invites us to think of this strange God like a father who welcomes home all wayward children (Luke 15:11-32). Therein lies the authority of the Bible for our lives today, or any time. The Bible is our source of knowledge of what our Creator is like and what God desires and seeks for creation.

Relationship with God Changes Us

The biblical story describes what happens to people who respond to God's offer of a loving relationship. They are drastically changed by entering that relationship. Scripture uses a great variety of words and stories to describe human life lived in an association with the Creator. Among the individual words are salvation, peace, blessing (happiness in its deepest sense), new creation, and love. Each of these terms is helpful, but at its core this is a new life centered in God's love and care. From that hub emerge spokes that reach out in different directions. Those who enter this relationship have a new understanding of themselves, relate to other people in a different way, and have a promise for their future.

The individual words are helpful, but so too are the stories of persons who become God's friends. In the Old Testament there are many stories of how such people prosper in this life. David is a prize example of this. He seemed to be successful in everything he did—at least until he violated his relationship with God. But the Old Testament qualifies the view that life becomes a bed of roses once you have faith in God. Job is, of course, the classic story of how the righteous suffer for no apparent reason. (For more on this topic, see chapter 6.)

The New Testament offers its share of stories of lives changed by this relationship. Little Zachaeus has his life turned upside down by Jesus' unexpected offer of friendship with him

(Luke 19:1-10). Paul's story is similar. The point is that association with one's Creator quite literally makes new people of us. We are, in Paul's words, "a new creation" (2 Corinthians 5:17). Or, to use Jesus' words in the Gospel of John, we are "born again" or born this time "from above"—that is, from God (John 3:1-15).

The Bible makes clear that we humans become locked into a kind of life in which we understand ourselves to be independent of God. The Bible calls that kind of life sin. Sin is what we do but, more importantly, it is what we are. By nature, we are creatures separated from the one who created us. The power of that sin (separated life) prevails in human cultures. So the inclination to think and live separate from God is more powerful than our weak ability to decide otherwise.

The new life in a loving relationship with God overcomes that separation. Consequently, the Bible makes a good deal out of God's forgiveness, mercy, and grace (that is, unearned love). Hosea expresses that kind of forgiveness in vivid terms that equate it with God's very being: "the Holy One in your midst" (11:1-9). Paul puts it in heavier theological language in Romans 3:21-26. He establishes the universal power of sin in the first two chapters of Romans, and then he writes of God's "righteousness"—that is, of God's nature to set right the relationship with humans. "Divine forbearance" motivates God "to pass over the sins previously committed." However it may be expressed, the biblical story of faith highlights God's act in Christ to release us from the bondage of a life separated from God.

The Bible is our authority for understanding the new kind of life that emerges from a relationship of love with God. To describe the quality of that new life is difficult. It goes beyond most of what our words and stories can express. But it might be summarized by saying that this new life is what God always intended life to be. In that sense it is what the Gospel of John calls "eternal life" or "abundant life." It is life with a particular quality that shares something with the Eternal One.

That New Life Results in Moral Behavior

Related to God in love, we share God's values. This means that we share God's concern for human welfare and the divine persistence in trying to nurture the common good among us. That is the reason the Bible is filled with "commandments." In the biblical story of faith, God guides the people in very specific ways. God informs them of what the divine heart holds dear: justice, righteousness, and peace. The biblical story does not mince words about God's frustration with those who refuse to understand this (read Amos for a good example). We can see God is committed to the improvement of human life and society.

Jesus offers the same commitment. He not only teaches God's values, but he also lives them. Jesus' associations with the lowly, the "throw away" people of society, for instance, demonstrate God's commitment to them and to all people.

We must be careful here. Living God's values depends on our situation, our social context. What Christian morality means is shaped by the society in which we live. The Old Testament, for instance, has lots of laws and case studies of righteous living that are defined in terms of a culture that is very different from our own (see chapter 6 for a discussion of the Old Testament). The divorce regulation in Deuteronomy 24 mentioned earlier was really ordered to protect the integrity of women disowned by their husbands. Literally, it is hardly relevant to us in our society. Yet it does demonstrate a compassionate concern for women.

In a similar manner, laws about leaving some of the harvest in the field for travelers and the needy (Deuteronomy 24:19-22) provided a social welfare system in an agricultural society. It still might be a good idea today but, practically, it is not much help for our urban homeless and hungry.

The moral injunctions in the New Testament are much the same, although the culture is a different one. They provide moral guidance for Christians in that day and in that cultural setting. Read, for instance, Paul's advice regarding meat offered to idols in 1 Corinthians 8:1-13. When is the last time you found such meat in the supermarket?

When it came to the question of how this new life in relationship with God was to be put into practice, the biblical writers spoke specifically and concretely in terms of the issues of their day. It would not have helped readers if the writers had simply advocated broad general principles. Literally, then, many of the moral injunctions of the Bible are not helpful to us in our very different cultural setting.

But this is not to say that the moral teachings of the Bible have no relevance for us. As we have seen, there are general principles that do have meaning today. Many transport easily from the biblical times and cultures to any time and culture. The commandment to love others is a golden thread stretched across the Bible's pages (see Deuteronomy 6:4-5, Leviticus 19:18, Mark 12:29-31, and 1 Corinthians 13). Justice and kindness (see Micah 6:8) are basic divine values that are timeless for any culture.

We need to be careful, however, about determining just what is a biblical moral principle. We are liable to read our own preferences into such decisions. This is where the role of the community of faith comes in interpreting the Bible. The identification of a biblical moral principle needs to be a community decision, not just an individual one. Notwithstanding the issues in identifying these moral principles, the biblical story makes some fundamentals evident (such as love of neighbor) and thereby offers us guidance for living our faith.

Furthermore, the specific moral teachings model for us ways by which we think through the connection between our new life with God and our daily behavior. Those specific instructions do not always directly relate to our situations, but they show us how to think about morality. Paul's discussion of eating food that had first been offered to idols, for example, shows us a basic way of making moral decisions. Paul demonstrates a compassion for the "weaker" person that prevents him from acting without considering how his actions will affect others (1 Corinthians 8:13). We ought, therefore, to study these teachings carefully to discern how the Hebrew people, the Jewish people, and the first Christians thought about morality. Learning how to make moral decisions will equip us to live faithfully in the midst of all the new challenges facing us today.

Consequently, the authority of the Bible in matters of morality is complicated. On the one hand, many of the specific moral injunctions are not binding on us in detail. The description of the moral woman in 1 Timothy 2:8-15, for instance, has little value. To be sure, we would agree that a woman's good works are of more value than the clothes she wears (verse 10). But the general description of women seems more a reflection of the culture of the time than of God's will for our lives. On the other hand, the Bible is authoritative in terms of its basic moral principles that can be shown to be essential to who God is (love and justice, for example). Furthermore, the biblical story makes clear that moral living is vital to any Christian life, that it should be specific to our culture, and that there is a way of moral reasoning helpful for our lives.

God Demands Something and Gives Something

The three ways in which the Bible is authority for us may be summarized in two categories. On the one hand, the Bible's story of faith clarifies what it is God expects of us. On the other hand, it narrates God's constant love for us. The first category has sometimes been labeled "law" and the second "gospel." Those labels are useful but prone to misunderstanding.

The authority of the Bible in the first instance (what God demands) has the power to make us aware of our separation from God. Human life without God is what Scripture calls sin. In effect, this kind of life is a pretense to be something we are not. We are not creatures who are independent of our Creator. We cannot "make it on our own" without a loving relationship with God. When we try to live independently of God, we are like fish trying to climb trees. The biblical God is continually trying to help us understand this. The divine demands made of us are ways of helping us find our true identity as God's creatures.

But the biblical God continually offers us forgiveness, love, and mercy. God's goal is a relationship of love with us. Particularly in the Bible's climax in Christ, God makes it clear that we are accepted as part of the divine family. We are accepted in spite of our fumbling efforts to make ourselves acceptable to our Creator.

Divine demand and divine love work together to bring us into that new association with our Creator where we have new life. This new life is expressed in moral living. This is why we have two kinds of experiences when reading the Bible. At times we feel condemned—convicted of living incorrectly. When we read the Ten Commandments (Exodus 20:1-17) or Jesus' beatitudes (Matthew 5:3-12), for instance, we are liable to feel hopeless about ourselves. But when we read "I have loved you with an everlasting love" in Jeremiah 31:3, we hear words of comfort and assurance. In John 3:16, Jesus declares, "God so loved the world that he gave his only Son." We know there is hope for us when we read these words.

Thus the Bible's authority is experienced in two very different ways. But both work to bring us back into a loving relationship with our Creator.

What Can We Expect of the Bible?

What is the Bible? It is an ancient book from a number of different cultures, containing a collection of community documents in many different literary forms. Taken together, the documents tell a single story of faith in a God who seeks a relationship with humans. With that understanding of the Bible in mind, in what sense is the Bible authority for our lives? It provides us a source of truth to understand the God who seeks a relationship with us. It informs us of how a new relationship of love with God changes us, and how that life change issues in moral behavior.

So What Difference Does It Make?

If this description of the Bible and its authority is sound, what difference does it make for reading Scripture? This question anticipates much of what concerns this book in the following chapters. But for now a number of conclusions may already be clear.

We read the Bible for what it has to say about God, our relationship with God, and how we live in that relationship. Notice that this view draws a pretty clear line between what we can and cannot expect from the Bible. We can expect the Bible to make a fundamental difference in our understanding of God and of ourselves. We cannot expect the Bible to tell us all the truth there is to know in this world, but only the most fundamental and important truth. The Bible is not a source of scientific truth. It does not tell us which form of government is the best, nor does it prescribe our membership in a particular political party. It can help us with moral questions, but it is not an answer-book for all our contemporary dilemmas.

The expectation that the Bible provides us with truth about the origin of our cosmos continues to be controversial. That issue is a good example of proper and improper expectations of the Bible. The Bible clearly states a faith perspective on creation. God is the originator and sustainer of all that is. But Genesis 1–2 do not provide us a basic science lesson in *how* God created the cosmos. Those chapters are part of the Bible's faith story and are meant to express the belief that everything is rooted in God. The effort to construct a "creationism" to rival modern views of evolution out of the first two chapters of Genesis expects something of the Bible it cannot deliver.

The view of the cosmos underlying the creation stories is a very different one from our contemporary understanding. The cosmos pictured in Genesis is an embryo in a womb filled with water. In the book of Psalms, those chaotic waters are called "the deep" (for example, Psalm 33:7 and 135:6). The earth is a flat disk held up by pillars (see Psalm 75:3), and the sky is a dome over the earth on which the heavenly lights travel (Genesis 1:17). The writers expressed their communities' faith in God's role as creator, but did so within the context of their understanding of the cosmos at that time. The faith affirmed in the passage tells us something important about believing in God. But the image of the cosmos is obsolete and frankly inferior to our scientific knowledge of what lies out there beyond our world. Do not expect the Bible to teach you science.

Do expect the Bible to teach you about yourself in a fundamental way. Self-understanding is one of the Bible's important contributions to us. It teaches us about our origin in God's creative work, our propensity to try to live without God, our possibilities for a life in harmony with God's original intent for us, and our eventual destiny with God. In this way, what the Bible has to say about God is limited to what we need to know in order to live in relationship with our Creator. The Bible does not probe the mystery of God's being. What it does tell us, however, is the "heart" of God (John 1:18). That may be all we really need to know.

Finally, we expect the Bible to teach us all we need to know about salvation. That is the way the church has often expressed its view of biblical authority. Salvation means that life with God that has been the center of our discussion in this chapter. We can expect the Bible to teach us about a right relationship with God.

But this proposal for understanding the Bible and its authority differs radically from others that we hear and read about. That raises the question of the various interpretations of the Bible that are afoot in our society today. What are we to make of these different views?

Chapter Three ―――――――――

Why So Many Different Interpretations?

ALL FOUR OF THE GOSPELS REPORT Jesus entered the Temple in Jerusalem and drove out the money changers stationed there. The Gospels of Matthew, Mark, and Luke each report that this incident occurred at the conclusion of Jesus' ministry (Matthew 21:12-13, Mark 11:15-17, and Luke 19:45-46). His opponents would soon arrest, try, and crucify him. The Gospel of John, however, tells this same story early in Jesus' ministry (John 2:13-17). Except for his participation in the wedding at Cana (John 2:1-11), his actions in the Temple were his first public appearance.

This fascinating difference between the Synoptic Gospels (Matthew, Mark, and Luke) and John has intrigued biblical interpreters. (The first three Gospels are called "Synoptics" because they share a common view of Jesus' ministry. *Synoptic* means to "see together" or have a common perspective.) Some solve the difference between the Synoptics and the Gospel of John by claiming that Jesus cleansed the Temple on two different occasions. He did it once early in his ministry and again just prior to his arrest. But other interpreters argue that the Gospel writers are responsible for the difference. For some reason the author of the fourth Gospel placed the event where we find it in John's story of Jesus. These interpreters often propose that John revised the chronological order we find in the Synoptics in order to focus attention on the symbolic quality of Jesus' cleansing of the Temple. Jesus' whole ministry would be a "cleansing" of the established religion of his day and place.

The different interpretations of Jesus' cleansing of the Temple exemplify the variety of ways in which Christians read the Bible. The two explanations for the location of this story suggest two different approaches to Scripture. In the first case, Scripture is taken on its word. If the Bible has two stories of Jesus' actions in the Temple at different periods in his ministry, then Jesus must have repeated this act a second time. In the second explanation,

Scripture is approached from a critical perspective. The word *critical* in this case simply means "analytical." It assumes that the writers of the Gospels exercised freedom in their telling of the story in order to stress certain themes.

Why are there such very different approaches to the Bible that result in conflicting interpretations? A response to this question requires that we travel through several related questions in order to get a better picture of contemporary biblical interpretation.

How Does the Bible Gain Its Authority?

The previous chapter drew clear lines between the areas in which the Bible is authority and the areas in which we should not expect it to provide us a source of truth. But another question lurks in the shadows of the topic of biblical authority. How does the Bible gain its authority among us? What is the process by which we come to understand the Bible as a source of truth for Christian life and faith?

Does the Bible Come Packaged in Authority?

Some Christians argue that the Bible's authority is within itself. The Bible's authority is intrinsic, they say. That means that its sovereignty is within its contents. The most we can do is accept or dismiss what the Bible is. In other words, the Bible claims its authority by virtue of what it is and teaches.

This view has several strengths. First, it acknowledges the power of the words of Scripture. The Bible is a powerful book. It can change lives with its message. The biblical documents make some mighty claims. Among them is the claim that the story it tells affects the eternal destiny of humans (see, for example, 1 Corinthians 1:18).

Second, the view that the Bible carries within itself its own authority leads us to take the biblical message seriously. Say you were presented with the constitution of the apartment house into which you have just moved. That document has authority. You will take its words very seriously, for they will influence your life in your new home. Today, traditional sources of authority are taken with less and less seriousness. To be introduced to a book that is in itself authoritative prevents our dismissing it as some outdated document from the past.

But the view that the Bible comes already packaged in authority also has some weaknesses. Is that really the way the Bible gains its authority among us?

Do We Wrap the Bible in Authority?

The alternative to the first view claims that we ourselves give the Bible its authority. It is not so much a matter of the internal authority of the Bible, but how we regard that book. We ourselves wrap the Bible in authority. This second approach to the Bible assumes two important facts.

First, something only becomes authority by virtue of a community's deciding it will have that authority. All authority arises from a group's agreement that something or someone will function as a source of truth for them. This is the way in which civil authority is established. We decide that the police, for instance, will have authority in our community. We will respect and obey them. For the sake of good order in the neighborhood, the police are given power. However, such authority can be withdrawn. In recent years, we have witnessed neighborhoods, even entire cities, in which residents have denied police their influence. They have done so because the police have abused their power and lost the respect they might have once had. Authority resides in some one or something by virtue of a community's assigning them or it such importance.

In the case of the Bible, the church decides that this collection of documents will have authority over its beliefs and life. The community of faith wraps the Bible in the cloak of authority. A nation's constitution is adopted by the agreement of a body of representatives of the people. The document has no status whatsoever until a vote is taken and the people agree that it will be their governing document. The church has so voted to grant authority to Bible. The church, of course, did so because it believed that it was guided to this decision by the Holy Spirit.

Whether or not this process of granting authority to the Bible is the way it actually happens is debatable. But some evidence favors such a process. Think, for instance, of the churches that have deliberately moved away from the Bible because they believe that it no longer functions the way it once did. Like the residents who deny the police authority, individual Christians and congregations have done much the same with regard to the Bible. They believe that it is no longer relevant to their lives.

Second, the view that the church gives the Bible its authority is based in history. Chapter 2 points out that the church actually created the canon out of a collection of documents. The Bible's origin as a document of authority is found in the gatherings of church leaders, called "councils." Those councils elevated the Bible to the status of a rule of faith and life. However, the councils simply ratified what congregations of the time were doing in their use of the biblical documents. But even those congregations had read and discussed these documents and reached the decision that they would henceforth provide those communities of faith with authority. So, the view that the church wraps the Bible in authority is sound in two ways. It is sound, generally, in that communities establish their own sources of authority. It is also sound in the sense that, historically, the church did make the Bible its authority.

Such a view, however, has several dangers. It may not clearly acknowledge the power of the biblical message. Compared with the first view (that the Bible comes already packaged in authority), this view may tend to diminish the Bible's own assertion of authority. Furthermore, humans make mistakes. We say the church decides the Bible will be authority. What if that is (and was) an error? The Bible's authority can be rescinded. The church can reverse its decision, as apparently some congregations have already done. Do we want the primary authority for our Christian lives vulnerable to human decision?

But the view that the church elevates the Bible to a place of authority also has several strengths. Clearly it acknowledges the Bible as a community book. It plants the Bible squarely in the life of the church. The consequence of this fact is that the Bible is always read and interpreted within a community context. It is difficult for me to interpret the Bible in isolation from my community of faith. Of course, community interpretation does not ensure freedom from the ever-present danger of error. The history of the church's interpretation of the Bible on issues such as slavery and the role of women makes us sensitive to the fact that the community itself may be wrong. Still, community interpretation helps us avoid some of the dangers of error.

It may not be such a bad thing that the Bible's authority is vulnerable to human decision. Perhaps it is better that the church as a whole and individual Christians have to go on deciding whether the Bible will continue to be a norm of faith. In a sense, this is what really happens. Suppose a congregation is deliberating whether or not to enter into a ministry to feed the hungry people of its neighborhood. Proponents of the proposal present biblical evidence that the people of God share their Lord's commitment to serving the needy. The congregation is forced to decide if the biblical teachings about feeding the hungry and clothing the naked are true for it. What they decide to do determines if the Bible is authority or not. On a daily basis, the church actually does decide if the Bible is going to serve as its resource for knowing God's desires for the people.

How Do We Approach the Bible?

These two views of the Bible's authority influence the way we approach Scripture. Both presuppose faith. The first view requires that we have faith in the Bible itself. It necessitates that we believe this document is authority for us. In the second view, we need faith to accept that God had a hand in the church's declaration the Bible would be authoritative for Christians. We read the Bible with the confidence that God led the church to create a canon out of these various documents. The first view cultivates faith in Scripture itself. The second view nurtures a faith primarily in God (or God's Spirit) and only secondarily in the Bible.

The first view also tends to strengthen an attitude toward Scripture as the flawless words of God. The Bible is its own authority. So the Bible must contain words from God. This approach will be described more fully in the next section. For now simply note that the first view tends to strengthen an uncritical approach to the Bible. Everything contained in Scripture is authority, at least in theory.

The second understanding of how the Bible gains authority is more likely to strengthen a critical or more analytical approach. The church decides the Bible is authority. So, in every reading of Scripture we will have to decide whether or not to confirm that decision. The second view opens the door to the possibility that some parts of the Bible are truth for us and, perhaps, other parts are not. Let's look at a hypothetical example.

Suppose that a Bible study group is looking at what Scripture has to say about divorce and remarriage. They read Mark 10:2-12 and begin discussing the material. They soon discover in verses 5 through 9 that Jesus seems to reject the endorsement of divorce found in the Old Testament (see Deuteronomy 24:13). Jesus claims this endorsement was written only because of "your hardness of heart" (Mark 10:5). Then Jesus clearly says remarriage after divorce is tantamount to "adultery" (Mark 10:11-12).

One member of the group, Susan, says, "Since it's in the Bible, it's true! Divorce and remarriage after divorce are both sins!" Another member, Jane, is not so sure. "Did Jesus really mean that a woman whose husband beats her on a daily basis cannot divorce him? I can't believe that Jesus would be that insensitive! And would Jesus deny that woman a chance at another marriage? I think not!" A third person suggests that Jesus may be objecting to the way divorce was practiced in his day. "If that's so," this member goes on, "then these words are not law for us today." Susan responds: "But you can't go through the Bible picking and choosing what you're going to accept. We either take it all or reject it all."

Susan holds something like the view that the Bible contains its own authority. Jane and the other speaker both seem to want to weigh the possibility that Jesus' words are not strict authority for us today. They are in fact deciding what authority these words will have for them. But Susan makes a very important point. If we are going to decide that the Bible is authority only in certain passages, on what basis do we make the distinction? We will address this question shortly. But before doing so, we must consider another question regarding biblical authority.

Is the Bible Inspired?

Closely associated with the Bible's authority is the claim that the Bible is inspired. What does that mean? In what sense is Scripture inspired? The previous chapter and this one have first discussed biblical authority because authority precedes the question of inspiration. In the church's history, the Bible was first thought to be authority before theories of its inspiration were advanced. During the late seventeenth century, the second generation of reformers were the first to develop those theories (for example, Johannes Andreas Quenstedt, 1617–88, and Abraham Calovius, 1612–86). They did so in order to support the authority of the Bible as they understood it. Nonetheless, views of the inspiration of the Bible are vital to the way we read it.

What Is Inspiration?

The word *inspire* means literally to "breath in." It is the opposite of *expire*, which means to "breath out." Inspiration has, however, taken on special religious meaning. Both the Hebrew and Greek words for spirit can also mean breath or wind. For instance, Genesis 1:2 says "a wind from God swept over the face of the waters." A footnote in the New Revised Standard Version of the Bible points out that the Hebrew in this verse could be translated "the spirit of God swept over. . . ." The "sound like the rush of a violent wind" at Pentecost suggests the presence of the Holy Spirit (Acts 2:2). So, the "breathing in" of inspiration has to do with God's Spirit entering a person or community.

The inspiration of the Bible claims that the presence and activity of the Holy Spirit were involved in its composition. The writing of the biblical documents was done under the guidance of God's Spirit. Even though the biblical writers were humans, they were directed in their compositions. The Bible's inspiration, then, is a faith statement about God's role in the writing process.

In What Sense Is the Bible Inspired?

Most Christians would agree that God inspired the writing of the Bible. But they disagree on what that means. To what degree did God control the writing? In what way did the Spirit guide the biblical writers? The often quoted passage in 2 Timothy 3:16, which claims that "all scripture is inspired by God," is not really relevant to the discussion. *Scripture* in this passage refers to portions of the Hebrew Scriptures (the Old Testament). The New Testament documents were not yet regarded as scripture when 2 Timothy was written.

Views of inspiration range over a wide spectrum. On the one extreme is the view that God "dictated" the words of the Bible. Christians who hold this view argue that every word in the Bible came from God. This position is sometimes called "literalism," meaning that the Bible is word for word the words of God. While some hold this extreme position, many modify it slightly. God inspired each word of the original documents. But in some cases those documents were tampered with and their divine quality at least partially qualified (see chapter 4).

At the far opposite extreme are those who understand inspiration in a far more general sense. God's Spirit initiated the original inspiration to write, but from that point on the writers were only guided in an ordinary way (like when we say a person had an "inspired" idea). So the Bible's words themselves were not from the Spirit, but the impetus and general meaning of a book were. The writer was inspired, for instance, to interpret an event as the action of God. The Spirit led the Hebrew people to interpret their escape from bondage in Egypt as God's intervention on their behalf. But the details of the story of their escape (for example, the ten plagues described in Exodus 7:14—12:32) were not necessarily from the Spirit. This view might be called "thematic inspiration," since it assumes the general themes of the Bible are inspired but not necessarily the words themselves.

The different views of inspiration clearly involve different understandings of the role of humans in the production of the biblical documents. At one end of the spectrum of views, the authors are secretaries taking dictation. At the other end, the authors are creators of the writing. They are inspired the way a poet might be inspired to write a sonnet. The issue comes down to the relationship of the divine and the human factors involved in the Bible's composition. Positions along the spectrum are too numerous to identify. But they include the distinction between the basic message and what results from cultural settings. In this case, Paul's message that God's righteousness was revealed in Christ to correct the relationship between humans and their Creator is inspired (Romans 3:21-26). However, his advice to the Roman Christians to obey "governing authorities" (Romans 13:1-7) arose out of his concern that the new Christian church cultivate a good relationship with the Roman Empire.

In recent years the understanding of the Bible as a collection of community documents (see chapter 2) has influenced views of inspiration. The writings contained in Scripture arose from specific communities of faith (Hebrew and Christian) and were addressed to those communities. Moreover, much of what is contained in the Bible is comprised of the communities' stories, sayings, and interpretations of events. Authors were actually putting into writing much of what was already present in their communities in oral forms. Therefore, some argue that inspiration needs to be understood as the presence and activity of God's Spirit within those communities.

Such a view of biblical inspiration is very helpful. Many of our modern views of inspiration tend to emphasize the individual authors. But those views of inspiration do not fit most of the biblical documents. Inspiration occurred within the community as a group experience. It was not simply an individual experience of being led by the Spirit. A contemporary parallel is found in books that attempt, in writing, to capture the stories found in a particular community. In these cases, an author interviews the elders of a community and records their stories of the past and impressions of the future. The finished work brings these stories together in a unified written form. The author's role, here, is comparable to that of the authors of biblical documents.

To be sure, there may be some exceptions. This kind of community inspiration is appropriate especially for the books of history in the Old Testament (for example, Exodus and 1 and 2 Samuel), as well as in Acts and the Gospels of the New Testament. It may be less appropriate for Paul's epistles, for instance. Paul, of course, draws on the traditions of the church. In 1 Corinthians 7:10-11, he writes that "not I but the Lord" commands. Yet later he writes about a related matter, "I have no command of the Lord but I give my opinion" (1 Corinthians 7:25). He concludes the discussion by asserting, "I think that I too have the Spirit of God" (1 Corinthians 7:40). Paul draws on the community's remembrance of Jesus' teachings. But he also ventures his own views, convinced that they are influenced by the Holy Spirit. Yet, we also know that his sense of having the Spirit is closely related to his life in the community of faith.

Perhaps the inspiration of the Bible was for the most part community inspiration. But we need not entirely exclude the Spirit's work with individual authors. How we finally resolve the question of the sense in which the Bible is inspired probably depends on our own experience with Scripture. It depends on the degree to which we have experienced Scripture speaking directly to our situation and needs. On occasions I have had a sense that a particular passage had my home address written all over it. When that happens to us, we are inclined to believe that the Spirit is at work in Scripture and in our reading of it. Those experiences are probably the basis on which we come to some clearer understanding of what biblical inspiration means. Should we think of inspiration, then, less in a broad and abstract doctrine and more in terms of what we learn from experiences with the Bible?

Is the Bible Free of Errors?

Views of inspiration lead to the question of the possibility of errors in the Bible. Those who hold a view of the direct and total inspiration of the Bible are inclined to speak of its "inerrancy" (a quality of being without error). In this view, error is not possible if God dictated every word of the Bible. Literalism usually includes such an assumption. On the other hand, those who hold the view of a "thematic inspiration" are likely to admit that the Bible does contain errors.

An example might be the conflicting views of Israel's conquest and settlement in Canaan described in the book of Joshua. According to Joshua 11:16, Israel conquered "all that land" through military might. Historians challenge this picture of Israel's migration into Canaan. They claim that the historical evidence suggests Israel's far more peaceful settlement among the Canaanites. Joshua is pictured as a military leader, when in fact he was probably more of a diplomat who negotiated with the inhabitants of the land. Which is a more accurate depiction of the historical events—that of the book of Joshua or the evidence available to us? A view that the Bible contains no errors necessitates that one accept the biblical account as true. But from the viewpoint of communal, thematic inspiration, the reader can acknowledge that the biblical picture may be a bit distorted or embellished.

The absolute inerrancy of Scripture has been modified among some into what is sometimes called "infallibility." Depending on with whom you speak, this modification means different things. But usually it claims that the Bible may have *insignificant* errors in it. The Israelites' exaggeration of their military might in the conquest of Canaan, for example, is not important. In matters of salvation, say some, the Bible never misleads readers. The Bible's essential message of God's work to bring humans into a new relationship with their Creator is worthy of our trust. In terms of what really counts, Scripture is God's message to us for a new life.

The questions of authority and inspiration are difficult. The range of views is considerable, and the two topics intermingle with one another like tiny threads in a tightly knitted piece of cloth. Where you come down on these complicated questions, again, depends very much on the orientation of the community of faith with which you are associated. Whatever answer you settle on, it will influence the way you read and understand Scripture. Much is at stake in weighing the relative merits of these views. But understanding the variety of interpretations of the Bible involves still another fundamental question.

Is the Bible the Word of God?

The Bible is often said to be the "word of God." The expression is really a metaphor. God's communication with us in the Bible is compared to the way we communicate with one another in words. The *word of God* means "God's message transmitted to humans." The origin of the metaphor is in the Old Testament.

Way back in Exodus we find reference to "the words of the Lord" (for example, Exodus 4:28 and 30). In the prophets we frequently hear "the word of the Lord came to . . ." (for example, Jeremiah 1:4).

We could rephrase our question this way: Is the Bible the means by which God communicates the divine message to us? But in the context of our world today, rephrasing it in that way leaves us facing a number of different answers. Each of these answers has supporters in various Christian churches. You will not be surprised that the views of biblical authority and inspiration discussed above all come into play in these alternatives.

The Word of God Is the Words of God

When some call the Bible the "word of God," they mean that the Bible's individual words are words God speaks to us. Such a view assumes the Bible is an absolute and literal authority. It also assumes that view of inspiration as God's dictation of the Bible to its authors. The Bible's freedom from all errors follows naturally from the other views. The expression "word of God" is simply a way of referring to the total package of God's individual words.

We have already summarized some of the strengths and weaknesses of this perspective in the discussion of the Bible as having its own authority. To regard the Bible as the words of God motivates us to take the Bible, in its entirety, very seriously. It leads to careful attention to the precise words in any text. As chapter 5 will argue, this is a strength in the interpretation of the Bible.

But such a view is plagued with having to do some interpretative gymnastics in the process of reading certain passages. Moreover, it begs off answering some tough questions. How, for instance, does one read a passage like Matthew 5:30: "If your right hand causes you to sin, cut it off and throw it away"? Does God sometimes exaggerate in order to make a point? Or, what of the difference between the Lord's Prayer in Matthew and Luke? Matthew 6:12 reads "forgive us our debts." Luke 11:4 says "forgive us our sins." Did God say it twice in different ways? Did God describe creation in two stories—one in Genesis 1:1-2:4a and the other in Genesis 2:4b-25? (The "a" and "b" after a verse number means that the verse has two or more parts.)

These questions are not intended to show disrespect for those who view the Bible as the words of God. Rather, they simply suggest that there are important and fundamental problems to be faced if one accepts this literalistic perspective.

The Word of God Is the Bible's Central Message

The second alternative for understanding the expression "word of God" applied to the Bible limits what is meant by *word*. Some argue that the essential message of the Bible is God's communication to us in the Bible. In this case, some aspect of the Bible is taken to be its primary emphasis. How one draws that line between the essential and the unessential is the prominent issue. Earlier, this discussion claimed that the efforts of God to reestablish a relationship with humans is the primary theme of the biblical story of faith. That theme might constitute the Bible's central message. Some such definition is necessary to hold this second proposition.

If the Bible's essential message is the word of God, then there are parts of the Bible that may not be God's word. Presumably two kinds of biblical material are pigeonholed in different categories. Those passages not relevant to the Bible's central message (the word of God) are put in the category of the words of humans. That decision would require determining what is relevant and what is not relevant. The Old Testament is very interested in genealogies. Family trees were important to Hebraic identity. Your ancestors shaped who you were. So, are they relevant to the Bible's central message? The genealogies of Jesus found in Matthew 1:1-16 and Luke 3:23-38 are clearly important as they establish Jesus' identity in those Gospels. They would have to be encompassed by the word of God.

In John 1:1-18, the "Word" refers to Christ. Therefore, some identify the word of God with Christ. The Bible is the word of God insofar as it proclaims God's revelation in Christ. The Bible's central message, in this view, is focused on Christ or, as Luther suggested, "what promoted Christ." Such an understanding of the Bible is commendable in many ways. But it raises several concerns. Where does the Old Testament stand in such a definition of the Bible's central message? Is the Old Testament the word of God in that we find Christ implied in some of its passages? Or, is it enough that the Old Testament is regarded as one long preparation for God's sending the divine Son? With a focus exclusively on Christ, it is difficult to give the Old Testament credit for the role it plays in the Bible's whole story of faith. (We will discuss the Old Testament more thoroughly in chapter 6.) Moreover, 3 John never mentions Christ. It is difficult to categorize this document if we strictly identify the "word of God" with Christ, the "Word."

This second alternative to understanding in what sense the Bible is the word of God occasions mention of another topic. People who hold this position are among those who find "a canon within the canon." They claim there is a central biblical teaching that is the basis on which we are to assess the importance of everything else. Such a proposal is wise and helpful. Most of us function with some sense of a central message when we read the Bible. Recall Jane, for example, in the imaginary discussion of Jesus' teachings on divorce and remarriage. She could not imagine Jesus' being insensitive to victims of abusive marital situations. Obviously she had other passages from which she derived a picture of the "true Jesus." For Jane these harsh words about divorce and remarriage do not harmonize with her image of Jesus. Jane has "a canon within the canon," even though it might be an unconscious one. Many of us are like her. We gain some impression of the Bible's central teaching and use that impression to evaluate the importance of every passage we read.

Reading the Bible with the assumption it contains a canon by which to evaluate its individual parts can be most helpful, but on one condition: If careful study and determination has gone into defining that inner canon. The problem is that many of us have not consciously undertaken the task of identifying such a central message. Furthermore, too many of our impressions of what the Bible teaches are gained as much from motion pictures (such as *The Ten Commandments*) or Sunday school teachers as they are products of careful biblical study. Whatever one believes to be the heart of the biblical message, that conclusion needs to be examined critically. It needs to be discussed within the community of believers. Otherwise, we are tempted to create the essential message of the Bible out of our own preferences—what we would really like the message to be.

The view that the Bible's central message is the word of God is a valuable one, in spite of the tough questions it poses. It avoids the difficulties of believing that the Bible is the collected words of God. It allows us to see the human quality of the Bible and acknowledge that the Bible arose from specific cultures at certain times and places.

The Word of God Comes through the Bible

Still a third option takes a different approach to the question of how the Bible is the word of God. Think of the issue in terms of a simple communication process. In communication there is a sender, a means, and a receiver. We might picture them this way:

Sender (God)——>Means (the Bible)——>Receiver (reader)

The first option (the word of God as the words of God) identifies the means of the communication with the sender. The second option (the word of God as the Bible's central message) identifies some part of the means of communication with the sender. The third option (the word of God as a message that arrives through the Bible) identifies the sender with the reception of the message. The first two options focus on biblical content. The third option focuses on the receiver's experience of the message.

To say that the word of God comes through the Bible, first of all, frees the divine word from the Bible. It affirms perhaps that the divine message most often comes through the Bible. But the word of God is free to come in other ways, say through the words of a friend who offers us forgiveness and healing. I know this experience very well. In what close friends have said to me I have sometimes recognized God's message for me at that moment. Consequently, if we hold this view, we need to be ready to receive God's message anytime and anywhere and from any source.

But as for the Bible, this way of understanding the word of God has to do with special moments of reading or hearing the Scripture. It takes seriously those experiences when individuals or communities believe God has spoken through a biblical passage to address their immediate situation. Preaching is sometimes understood this way. On the basis of a biblical text, the preacher speaks to the present condition of the congregation. If the sermon is effective, the congregation leaves believing that God spoke to them through the sermon.

A very definite kind of hearing or reading is identified as the word of God. That occasion may be difficult to articulate. It includes the sense that a message from beyond oneself and this world intrudes itself into our situation. Such a word may challenge or console us. It may guide or warn us. It may convict or forgive us. But it is a powerful and life-changing experience.

Again, this option, too, has much that is commendable. But, like the other two options, this one also has its own set of problems. Perhaps the most important is that the word of God is identified with a particular experience. Chapter 1 discusses some of the dangers of experience as a source of truth. They all apply here. Even if we think not just of individual experiences, but also of community experiences, the same dangers are nearby. Community experience, too, is susceptible to cultural influences and various moods. A discouraged congregation might hear a particular passage that condemns all who differ from it. Members of that congregation might take that to be God's word to them that reinforces their prejudices about others.

The view of the Bible as the means for the communication of God's word may also diminish attention to the whole biblical story. Certain parts of the Bible are more likely occasions for hearing or reading the word of God. But what do we do with the others? In other words, this third option may have some of the same problems as the view that the word of God is the Bible's central message. Unless one remains alert to the possibility that any biblical passage might be the medium of God's word, this view might tend to cut and paste together a new Bible—one with only the passages that are most likely to occasion the word of God.

What Then Shall We Say?

How is the Bible the word of God? You must make the decision. Do not assume that the three options just described exhaust the possibilities. Maybe you can find a way of carving out still other and more viable positions. But these three are answers that have been tested and employed in contemporary Christian thought about the Bible.

There is clearly another option of a more radical kind. The expression "word of God" is a solidly biblical metaphor for God's communication with humans. But maybe there are other more contemporary metaphors that would function just as well, if not better, in the era of the communication revolution. Thinking of the metaphor in terms of "the news of the Lord" might be helpful. Perhaps "God's connection" with us (like the connection with a computer network) can help us talk about the meaning of the Bible. All I suggest is that you think about ways of rephrasing "word of God" that make it meaningful for you.

There is a frequent and somewhat careless way in which people speak of the Bible as the word of God. It is one of those expressions that is likely to roll off our tongues without much thought about what we intend to say. This section on the Bible as the word of God hopes to facilitate your careful and conscious use of the expression.

Why So Many Interpretations?

The array of views of the Bible's authority, its inspiration, and its nature as the word of God may help us understand why there are so many different interpretations. The assumptions we make about the Bible determine how we approach it. In turn, how we approach a text results in how we interpret it. The variety of views on each of the three topics explored in this chapter means there will probably always be a variety of interpretations. Think of all the differences among those of us who call ourselves Christians. Is it any wonder that those differences are going to yield different readings of Scripture?

The alternative is not very attractive. We could all join one church and give the officials of that new church authority to interpret Scripture for us. We would simply take their word for the meaning of any passage. But the church tried that in the period before the reformation of the sixteenth century and before the invention of the printing press. Once everyone had a Bible in his or her own language, it became more difficult for church leaders to dictate interpretation of Scripture.

But maybe the vast number of interpretations is not all that bad. Perhaps the diversity of readings of Scripture is a resource from which we can learn and thus enrich our Christian lives. Two examples of how this works are already evident.

The first example includes the interpretations of the Bible by people in different cultures. Especially helpful are those who read the Bible in contexts of oppression and poverty. They enable us to see the freeing dimension to a good many passages that we have read, usually without noting such a message. For instance, have you ever noticed that Jesus' beatitude in Luke 6:20 reads simply, "Blessed are you who are poor"—not, "Blessed are the poor in spirit," as Matthew reports (Matthew 5:3)? Those of us who are of European descent and middle class have much to learn about our Bible from Christians in other nations and cultures. That includes subcultures within our own nation. African American Christians, for instance, have vastly enhanced the understanding of Scripture.

The feminist movement among Christians is another example of how a diversity of interpretations enriches us. It has produced some new and exciting ways of reading and understanding Scripture. Feminist readings cultivate our appreciation of the Bible simply by sharing what the Bible seems to say from the perspective of women. Feminist perspectives have helped me see the role women play in the Bible's story of faith and sensitized me to the way in which men have always been our biblical interpreters. (Chapter 7 discusses the feminist interpretation movement in some detail.)

Might we not learn from listening to one another more carefully and respectfully? What might we see in Scripture for the first time if we listen to the interpretations of a literalist or someone who reads the Bible with, let's say, a New Age perspective? It seems beneficial to draw on support from wherever we can find it, as the Bible is rich with meaning and possibilities for speaking God's word to us. We need to resist our temptation to label others and dismiss them. Groups of Christian interpreters of the

Bible are important for our reading of it. That includes groups whose approaches to Scripture differ markedly from our own. Christians are, after all, all one body with many parts (1 Corinthians 12:12-27). Let's use all the body's members in our effort to understand the Bible.

Chapter Four ──────────
Is Something Lost in Translation?

THE REVISED STANDARD VERSION (RSV) OF THE BIBLE was first published in 1952. I was a freshman in college at the time. Like most Protestants in the mid-twentieth century, I was familiar with the King James Version (KJV). Amid all of the differences the RSV introduced, one provoked the most outrage. Isaiah 7:14 was translated in part, "Behold, a young woman shall conceive and bear a son." Matthew 1:23 quotes that Isaiah verse. But there it was translated, "Behold, a virgin shall conceive and bear a son . . ." The translators of the RSV seem to have stolen away the Old Testament roots for the virgin birth. I participated in several heated conversations about the importance of the new translation of Isaiah. Eventually I learned that the Hebrew word in Isaiah 7:14 did not mean that the woman to whom the prophet refers was necessarily a virgin, but only that she was of an age capable of conceiving.

The New Revised Standard Version (NRSV) appeared in 1989. It has aroused its own controversy. One difference introduced by the NRSV is sure to stir discontent. The RSV continued the translation "his star in the East" in the story of the wise men's journey to find Jesus (Matthew 2:1-12). The NRSV, however, translates the ambiguous Greek phrase "his star at its rising" (Matthew 2:2). Since the wise men lived in the East and followed the star by traveling west, it makes little sense that the Greek could mean "his star in the East."

The English Bible is a translation of those three languages in which the original texts were written: Hebrew, Aramaic, and Greek. So, we English readers have but two choices. Either we learn those three ancient languages or we depend on translations. Can we trust the translators? Those involved in the translation of the RSV were charged with being faithless, even demonic! Most of us remain at the mercy of translators in reading Scripture.

What is lost in translation? The question is complicated because it involves understanding the Bible's own history as well as the process of translation. So before discussing translation itself, this chapter needs to consider the text in the original languages from which translators work.

How Did We Get the Bible?

The Bible's own history is a fascinating and complex one. If we understand it, we can better understand the translations of the Bible into English. This discussion will first sketch the process by which the biblical documents were written and circulated. Then we will ask what difference that process makes for those of us who rely on translations.

The Bible's History

The earliest stage of the Bible's history is buried deep in the recesses of history. Imagine the recovery of that history as the effort of detectives trying to solve a mystery. The mystery is how our Bible came to be.

The clues to the origin of the Bible are the ancient manuscripts that have survived through the centuries since their origin. Some of them were discovered buried among ancient books within monastery libraries, preserved in the dry climate of the Middle East. The oldest of these are fragments of books, sometimes little more that a portion of an original page. Some have pages missing. Others passages are so terribly marred that they cannot be read. The evidence also includes early translations into other languages, such as the "old Latin," portions of which may have been written in the second century, C.E. Another source of the earliest fragments of biblical documents are quotations of Scripture used by early Jewish and Christian writers such as Clement of Rome at the end of the first century, C.E.

From this evidence and other historical knowledge, biblical detectives have constructed a sketch of how the documents in our Bible originated. The sketch begins, of course, with the original documents as their authors produced them (called "autographs"). They were written by hand, most often on sheets of papyrus. Those sheets were made by pressing strips of the papyrus plant together to form individual leafs. The leafs were then glued together to produce scrolls. Later the leafs were bound together to form books.

Ancient writing used little of what we today take for granted. The original Hebrew, for instance, included no vowels in the words. Imagine learning to read words without vowels: mgn lrnng t rd wrds wtht vwls. A group of rabbis, called the "Masoretes," added vowels to the words so they could chant the texts. The evidence suggests that these rabbis wrote during the ninth through twelfth centuries, c.e. Scholarly detectives working with Old Testament passages need to decide which vowels make the most sense in the context in which a word is found. Did the Masoretes add the correct vowels?

Ancient writing also used little of what we call punctuation. Nor did it avail itself of spaces between individual words. Sentences ran together without benefit of end punctuation. No quotation marks were used, so sometimes it is difficult to know when an author is citing another writing or a common saying. Writing was a tedious chore, so authors frequently made use of abbreviations.

Using these same writing practices, the original documents were then copied so they could be shared with others. Soon there were copies of copies, and the originals were lost. Imagine the task of making a copy of one hundred and fifty psalms and doing it by hand. It was easy to make errors. By comparing ancient biblical manuscripts of the same passage, it is clear that some copiers (called "scribes") skipped lines and omitted words. Moreover, the scribes were not copy machines. They were humans with their own views and beliefs. Not surprisingly, they sometimes added their own views with a few well chosen words. They apparently also made some changes when they disagreed with what the biblical author had written (or the previous scribe had copied).

Something like this seems to have happened between verses 7 and 8 of 1 John 5. A scribe apparently wanted to widen the author's references to "three that testify." So, after verse 7 he added: "There are three that testify in heaven, the Father, the

Word, and the Holy Spirit, and these three are one." Then he prefaced verse 8, writing, "And there are three that testify on earth."

A considerable collection of ancient manuscripts have survived. But unfortunately they are copies of copies in every case. The Isaiah Scroll discovered at Qumran along the shores of the Dead Sea represents one of the best and earliest examples. Most of what we have are from the Common Era, centuries after original copies were written. The oldest New Testament fragment dates sometime in the first half of the second century, C.E., but it is a tiny piece of writing. There is little hope of ever uncovering an original autograph.

Solving the Mystery

Fortunately a specialized biblical study called "textual criticism" developed to investigate the evidence. These scholars are the detectives who pour over the ancient manuscripts and compare representatives of the same biblical book. They avail themselves of the findings of other scholars who are experts in the ancient languages. One of the benefits of our time is that contemporary scholars know considerably more about the languages in which the biblical documents were written than did their predecessors. Among the textual critics' contributions to our understanding of the earliest manuscript is their discovery of family resemblance among the surviving texts. They propose that a number of manuscripts were copied from the same source. So, these scholars construct a kind of "family tree" of the existing documents with certain of them showing the characteristics of the same parent.

Part of these scholars' skill and discipline is to read these ancient fragments. They must, of course, make decisions about how to divide a steady flow of lines into individual words. Suppose a manuscript includes "heisnowhere." Should we read "he is nowhere" or "he is now here"? They become skilled in the ancient languages, so that they can detect whether a sentence is a question or a statement.

The detectives of ancient manuscripts try to identify subtle indications of the relative value of each manuscript. Which gives us the closest possible representation of the original? They must sometimes deliberate about different readings of the same texts. For instance, the old copies of John 1:18 conclude with at least two different statements. Some manuscripts have "It is the only God, who. . . ." Others say, "It is the only Son, who. . . ." (In the NRSV, translators have combined the two: "It is God, the only son, who. . . .")

Students of the earliest manuscripts have developed some principles for making the hard decisions about which manuscript is most likely to provide the best representation of the autograph. When the manuscripts disagree with one another, they tend to favor the most difficult and problematic reading. They do so because the copiers liked to make difficult texts more understandable.

Examples of this practice are found in ancient texts of the Gospels. In this case, scribes liked to harmonize the four Gospels so that they all agreed. For instance, the Lord's Prayer in Luke 11:2-4 does not include the phrase from Matthew 6:10, "Your will be done, on earth as it is in heaven." But some old manuscripts of the Gospel of Luke include that phrase. In those cases, textual critics believe the scribes tried to complete Luke's version with additions from Matthew's. The more difficult reading in this case is the shorter one. It is usually easier to explain an addition than to account for a shortened reading.

After the textual critics have done their work, they assemble a complete text in the ancient language that comprises their best judgments. However, these texts are accompanied with elaborate footnotes that inform readers of the alternative possibilities found in the manuscripts. English readers get the most important of these in an annotated Bible. In the NRSV, when there is strong manuscript evidence for another reading than the one printed in the body of the text, there will be a footnote. Those usually begin with "Other ancient manuscripts read . . ." or "Other ancient authorities add. . . ." This means those of us who use English translations get condensed versions of the manuscript options over which the scholars have deliberated.

Translators work with the text assembled by the scholars who have studied all the existing manuscripts of documents included in the Bible. Translators stand on the shoulders of their colleagues who have done this preliminary work in textual criticism. Needless to say, with each new discovery of an ancient biblical manuscript, we may make some little progress toward having a text closer to what the original authors produced. That is why the Qumran discovery was so important for Old Testament studies. It gave the textual detectives considerably more evidence with which to work.

What Difference Does This History Make?

The mystery of the origins of the Bible and its solution at the hands of scholarly detectives are intriguing. But they may also raise a good many doubts about the adequacy of our translations. The translators must use the reconstruction of something that resembles the original writing (the autograph). Does that mean we cannot trust our Bible to be identical to what the writers produced? There is no doubt that understanding the Bible's history behind translations sobers our view of Scripture. A great many decisions have been made by students of the ancient languages and by textual critics. Since scholars too are human, those decisions may not always be sound.

The story of the Bible from original writings to the constructed texts used by translators issues a warning. There are good reasons for suspecting a literal view of Scripture. The previous chapter mentioned that some Christians believe only the original documents were literally inspired by God word for word. Because of the history sketched above, such believers recognize that a degree of word-for-word inspiration has been lost in the process of copying and recopying. We may be wise to look for general meaning and thematic inspiration rather than literal precision.

The path between the original writing and the reconstructed text on the translators' desks is fraught with dangers. But we have two good reasons for believing that the Bible with which the translators work is trustworthy. The first is the enormous amount of scholarly work entailed in the study of the languages and the representations of the autographs. I am always impressed by the detailed analysis the textual critics have done with each and every biblical passage. All the representations of a passage have been studied intensely and thoroughly. Every possibility for accounting for the differences among them has been carefully weighed. The best of human scholarly endeavor has gone into this kind of work. To be sure, it is not free of possible error. But that possibility has been minimized to the degree humans can ever diminish the danger of mistake.

The second reason for trusting the work of textual criticism is a matter of faith. As Christians, many of us believe God some how inspired and led the writing of the original documents. Surely we can believe, too, that God has been involved in their preservation. We can believe the Spirit has been at work in the process of the copying and handing on of the manuscripts. We can believe the Spirit has guided the work of the scholarly detectives who put together the reconstructed text from the evidence that has survived the passage of time. In other words, faith in the Bible entails some faith in the process of its journey through time to us. But the Bible's story involves still another step between its origin and us.

Translations of the Bible

Our understanding of the translation process involves consideration of a number of questions. For our purposes, those include at least these four: What is translation? What questions must translators answer? Why do some Bibles include books not found in others? Which translation is the best?

What Is Translation?

Translation is the process of producing in one language the sense of words from another language. It is a process of transferring meaning from one language to another. Obviously, it involves understanding the meaning of the first language and an ability to reproduce it in a second language. Language is a feature of a culture. So invariably translation involves knowledge not only of languages, but also of the cultures of which the languages are a part. Translators work on the bridge between two cultures and their respective languages. They run back and forth, if you will, from one end of the bridge to the other. They carry the language and culture of one side of the gulf to the other and back again.

Translators must strike a balance between two values: faithfulness to the original words on the one hand, and easy reading in the second language on the other. For instance, an absolutely literal translation of a Biblical passage would not make for good English reading. This is a literal translation of John 3:16: "For thus loved the God the world that the son the only born one he gave that all the believing ones into him may not perish but have life of the age." Translators try to find a way to preserve the original meaning and still produce an English version that is easy to read.

English translations of the Bible are of several different kinds. Some are the work of a committee of scholars, while others are the product of a single translator. Some lean toward the literal meaning of original languages and some toward making the translation good and readable English. In reproducing the biblical languages into contemporary English, translators seek what is called "dynamic equivalences" of the Bible's words. The absolute equivalent (that is the literal translation) may not be the best choice of words. Instead they look for English words that are functionally equal to the original ones.

Look at Matthew 5:15 as an example. Jesus points out that no one puts a lamp under what the NRSV skillfully translates a "bushel basket." The Greek word is actually a prescribed amount of grain. It was approximately 8.75 liters, nearly a "peck" or about one-quarter of a bushel. Matthew's Greek says no one puts a lamp under a container that holds a peck of grain. But most of us do not know what a peck is any more. (I had to look it up in my English dictionary.) The translators seek a container whose contents constitute a measured amount of something. "Bushel basket" is the dynamic equivalent of the Greek word and what it meant in the culture of the first century, c.e.

Translations involve various degrees of making the ancient languages contemporary. So-called contemporary translations go further in their freedom from the original languages than does the NRSV. At the far extreme are paraphrased translations, such as *The Living Bible*. These take great liberties with the original languages in hope of making them understandable. "Amplified Bibles" try to give readers a number of translations at each passage through a series of phrases and sentences.

What Questions Must Translators Answer?

Translators must respond to the question of how far to move away from the original languages for sake of contemporary reading. But they also face a number of other questions as well.

The first of these involves the effort to preserve the value of earlier translations. To what degree should a contemporary translation attempt to conserve the virtues of its predecessors? The alternative is to ignore earlier translations and work only from the most recent original language construction produced by the textual critics.

Translators who want to produce a new "version" tend to work with one eye on Hebrew, Aramaic, and Greek texts and the other on the "authorized versions" preceding the current translation. Authorized versions originated with the KJV translation, first published in 1611. It was valued so highly that it became the regular translation used in Christian worship and in private reading. In time the KJV was followed by the American Standard Version published in 1901. That in turn was followed by the RSV and now the NRSV. All of these versions were formally endorsed by ecumenical church bodies in their time.

The KJV is without doubt a literary masterpiece of Elizabethan English. Its sheer beauty sustained its use for centuries and influenced a great deal of Western literature and art. Even at the close of the twentieth century, the New King James Version was published. In spite of its accomplishments, the KJV translation suffers a number of significant weaknesses. Its language is antiquated. The understanding of the ancient languages on which it was based has been surpassed in the intervening centuries. The KJV Bible was essentially a translation of the Latin Vulgate, and we now have access to vast numbers of other manuscripts on which to base translations. The authorized versions that have succeeded the KJV are far more effective translations in nearly every way.

Versions always honor their predecessors by trying to represent to contemporary readers what earlier authorized versions include. So, for instance, the RSV dropped the seventeenth century use of "thee," "thou," "hast," and other outdated words. However, in language addressed to God (for instance, in prayers) the RSV preserved that language. Psalm 8:1 is translated (in part): "How majestic is thy name in all the earth." The NRSV drops all such language. Its rendering of the same verse reads: "How majestic is your name. . . ." Translators must always decide to what degree they will continue the language and expressions of popular translations preceding them.

Translators must also decide how to handle certain passages that are problematic. There are a number of passages that can no longer be represented as part of their respective books but they also cannot be ignored. Two examples in the Gospels demonstrate the problem.

The ending of the Gospel of Mark is represented in three different ways in the ancient manuscripts we now have. The first way ends the Gospel with 16:8: "And [the women] said nothing to anyone, for they were afraid." The "shorter ending" follows 16:8 with two statements: The women told others what they had experienced, and the risen Christ sent the disciples out to proclaim "eternal salvation." The "longer ending" includes verses 9 to 20, which recount several stories of Christ's appearances to the disciples.

Most scholars now consider the abrupt ending at verse 8 the best representation of the original. It is clearly the most difficult of the three representations. But there is some evidence in favor of each of the other two endings. The translators of the NRSV end the chapter with verse 8, but append "The shorter ending of Mark" in double brackets after verse 8. Then verses 8 to 10 are printed in a footnote. The RSV has both the shorter and longer endings in the footnotes.

Another example of a problematic passage translators must decide how to handle is the story of the woman accused of adultery and brought to Jesus. It is most often found in John 7:53—8:11. The ancient manuscripts, however, actually have this story in four different places: In the Gospel of John it is found in three different locations (following 7:52, 7:36, and 21:25). But some other ancient Greek manuscripts tell the story after Luke 21:38. Most scholars think the episode is part of the church's oldest memories of Jesus. But this story seems to have floated from place to place both in John and even beyond it into Luke. How should translators present this story? The RSV relegated it to a footnote after John 7:52 and mentions its other locations. The NRSV translators decided to put it in the main body of the text in double brackets accompanied by an explanatory footnote.

In passages such as these, translators have to decide how to inform English readers of the uncertainty of particular passages. Such passages present problems in terms of their accuracy in representing the original writing. But they are, nonetheless, important. Some of the passages are beloved and well known (for example, the woman taken in adultery). Simply to pass over them does both scholarship and contemporary readers an injustice.

But translators must also sometimes make decisions about such seemingly insignificant things as punctuation. Textual critics propose such punctuation in the text they reconstruct. But translators must decide whether or not to accept those proposals. A simple example is found in John 1:9. Does the phrase "coming into the world" have to do with "the light" or with "everyone"? The NRSV reads, "The true light, which enlightens everyone, was coming into the world." But a footnote acknowledges the alternative: "He was the true light that enlightens everyone coming into the world." Both of these translations are legitimate renderings of the Greek.

Most English translations read Isaiah 1:18 as a statement, including "though your sins are like scarlet, they shall be as white as snow." But other translators believe that this sentence is more likely a sarcastic question: "though your sins are like scarlet, shall they be as white as snow?" Scholars must decide which type of sentence fits this context in Isaiah. In cases such as this, translators are handling sensitive matters. To translate this passage as a question has significant implications for the life of the church. On the other hand, there are good reasons to do so on the basis of the sense of the larger passage.

The question of how to punctuate a translation surfaces another question. Translators must ask how to keep their work from becoming an interpretation of a passage. Every translation is to some degree invariably an interpretation. Translators must decide what a passage means if they are going to reproduce it in another language. That is, they must understand the passage. But translation must not become a means of advancing a particular interpretation. The proposal that Isaiah 1:18 is a question supposes a certain interpretation of the passage. Probably one of the reasons that the passage is generally not presented as a question is that translators regard such a decision too interpretative. Their task is to arrive at a general sense of a passage and render that into English without imposing their own interpretation on it. Readers of English translations are, however, wise to remember that no expression of the original languages into English is without some interpretation.

Another question has become crucial for English translators of the Bible: What should they do with language that seems to include only men? The nrsv is the first of the authorized versions to attempt even a moderate move toward "gender-inclusive language" (that is, language that includes both men and women). For instance, in the New Testament the nrsv translators add "sisters" after the word "brothers" (or "brethren") in order to make the Greek inclusive (for instance, 1 John 2:9). In Matthew 25:40 "the least of these my brothers" is rendered "the least of these who are members of my family." In all cases, the nrsv includes a footnote stating what the Greek actually says. In some cases, however, this effort to be gender inclusive has produced some strange effects. For example, Matthew 2:16 says that Herod's agents "killed all the children in and around Bethlehem who were two years old or under . . ." Herod's deed was dastardly, to be sure, but at this passage the Greek clearly says he had all male children killed. Perhaps the well-intentioned efforts of the translators have, in this case, distorted the original language.

Other translations go much further. They attempt to make language that speaks both of Christ and God gender-inclusive. The nrsv seeks words that include all people regardless of gender. The more radical translations assume that inclusion necessitates eliminating male preference from all biblical language. So, for instance, one such effort speaks of Christ, not as God's son, but of God's "child." These translators try to avoid the use the metaphor of God as king, because it is exclusively male. Consequently, "the kingdom of God" becomes "the dominion of God."

This difficult and controversial question exemplifies how translators must be sensitive to current changes in language. In contemporary North American culture, masculine language is not always assumed to include women. But the biblical language arose from a society in which men were dominant and women were regarded as subordinate to them. How far from the biblical language should the translators move in order to accommodate cultural changes in language? Translators are doomed to criticism no matter how they respond. Is it more important to represent the original language accurately or to provide readers with a sense of being included among those whom the Bible addresses? Note, too, that translators in this case consider the way in which the Bible is received in contemporary culture. They are committed to a scholarly enterprise but also to the church's ministry through the Bible's reading.

Needless to say, Bible translators have a difficult and sensitive task. They juggle a number of different questions while deliberating how to give us a faithful English translation.

Why Do Some Bibles Include Books Not Found in Others?

This question arises from the fact that the Roman Catholic and Orthodox churches use Bibles that include the "Apocryphal" (meaning "hidden") or "Deuterocanonical" (that is, "secondary canon") books. The list of these books varies somewhat among the Roman Catholic, Greek Orthodox, and Slavic Orthodox Bibles. The books are documents that are not part of the Hebrew Bible, but they were included in the translation of the Hebrew Scriptures into Greek.

The translation into Greek of what we call our Old Testament was done sometime between 200 B.C.E. and C.E. 50. The translation is often identified as the "Septuagint" (meaning *seventy* and commonly abbreviated LXX). An ancient legend told how seventy Jewish elders accomplished the task of producing the Hebrew Scriptures in the Greek language. The task was apparently necessary, because Jews living outside of Palestine knew Greek better than Hebrew. Moreover, they wanted their Scriptures in the language of their culture for the sake of propagating Judaism.

The Septuagint includes all the books of the Old Testament. But it also includes a number of other books which are of two kinds. The first includes additions to biblical books. For instance, the Septuagint includes additions to the books of Esther and Daniel. Beyond these appendages to biblical books, the Septuagint also includes other writings, including 1 and 2 Maccabees, Judith, and Tobit. Along with the Scriptures themselves, these documents were popular among Jews who lived beyond the borders of their homeland. Moreover, what the Jews regarded as Scripture was still flexible when the Septuagint was produced. Except for the Torah (the first five books of our Old Testament), the Jewish canon was not yet defined. That process began toward the end of the first century, c.e. When the process of establishing the Jewish canon was completed, it did not include these extra writings found in the Septuagint.

But the Septuagint became the Old Testament of the earliest Christian church. Since Greek was the common language of Roman Empire, the church used the Greek translation of the Hebrew Scriptures. Some of the quotations of the Old Testament found in the New Testament appear to be based on the Septuagint (for example, Romans 15:9). The division of the church between the West and the East (around c.e. 1000) resulted in today's differences between Roman Catholic and Orthodox Bibles.

The documents, sometimes called the Apocrypha, were included in the Latin Vulgate, the official translation for Roman Catholic church made by St. Jerome in the fourth century. The reformers of the seventeenth century, however, objected to them. Their objections arose because of the reformers' opposition to certain teachings of the Roman Catholic Church, some of which were supported by passages in this collection of books. For example, Roman Catholic teachers of the time appealed to an early idea of purgatory in 2 Maccabees 12:43-45. They also used Tobit to support the view that human salvation was earned through good deeds. Luther and other of the reformers objected to these doctrines and, hence, objected to the Apocrypha. In his translation of the Bible into German, Luther relegated these books to the end of the Bible and labeled them "Apocrypha" to diminish their value. *Apocrypha* then came to mean "separate" and "not canonical." At the Council of Trent in 1546 the Roman Catholic church formally declared that these writings were "deuterocanonical." In doing so, the church decided the translations were a secondary but inspired canon, valuable but not on an equal status with the primary canon. Hence, official Roman Catholic Bibles include these documents. But Bibles used by Protestants often do not.

The Septuagint is important for a number of reasons. It helps us understand Jewish faith and thought in the period just before the rise of Christianity. Furthermore, it is a valuable source used by Old Testament textual critics. More important, it was the first Christian Bible. Even before the New Testament was acknowledged as canon, Christians read and studied the Septuagint.

For these reasons as well as others, the reading and study of the Apocrypha or deuterocanonical books, which are not always part of our Bible, are important. Christians have long found in them a resource for life and faith. To be sure, they are not to be accorded a status equal to the Bible itself. But like our Roman Catholic sisters and brothers, we can treat them as valuable without diminishing the worth of the Bible itself. For instance, the story told in 1 Maccabees witnesses to the courage and faith of the Jewish people under persecution. Reading it helps us find new courage and empowerment for our Christian witness.

Please note that these books are not the source for some of the Roman Catholic views occasionally falsely attributed to them. They do not, for instance, provide the basis for the perpetual virginity of Mary and her eventual ascension into heaven. Those views arose from Papal decrees and not from the Apocrypha.

Which Translation Is the Best?

Bookstore shelves are filled with a variety of translations. Which is the best among them? Rather than deciding which translation is best for you, let's mention some of the considerations to keep in mind when selecting an English Bible.

What *you* want and need for Bible reading is the first and obvious consideration. Young people need a translation that is easily read, free of archaic language. They are more likely to find a contemporary translation a good introduction to the Bible.

The Good News Bible and the Contemporary English Version (both published by the American Bible Society) are good choices. The New Living Translation is a much better option than its predecessor, *The Living Bible*.

Suppose, on the other hand, you are an adult Christian already acquainted with the Bible. In that case, you may be interested in a translation that more faithfully represents the original languages. You want a translation that may not read as easily as a newspaper but one that will offer you a clear translation of the ancient texts. There are many options for such readers. The New Revised Standard Version and the Revised Standard Version are among the best. Others include *The Jerusalem Bible*, The New International Version, and The New American Standard Version.

You may want to compare translations. If so, there are "parallel Bibles" that include a number of different translations side by side. The *Complete Parallel Bible with the Apocrypha/Deuterocanonical Books* presents four such translations. Even if you do not read Greek or Hebrew, "interlinear" Bibles present the original language with a literal English translation in a parallel column with one of the contemporary English translations. Those literal translations may prove helpful to you.

Another thing to consider is the difference between translations done by a committee and those done by independent scholars, such as Eugene Peterson's *The Message: The New Testament in Contemporary Language*. These translations are interesting and can help us reexamine from a different perspective passages we thought we knew. For the most part, however, committee translations are preferable. The teams of scholars correct one another, debate difficult decisions, and finally come to a consensus on how a particular passage should be put into English. The process lessens the impact of interpretation on translation, even though it does not entirely eliminate it.

Finding What Has Been Lost

Is something lost in translation? Yes! There is no denying that translations cannot capture the whole of the original languages. But that which is lost can be found!

We can trust the textual critics and translators of our Bible. They have devoted their lives to the study of Scripture. Because of their devotion, we can be assured that the central message of the Bible is preserved in our translations. What is most important in the Bible is not lost in translation. What is sometimes lost are nuances of meaning, subtleties of expressions, and the fine points of the stories or speeches. But some of them can be found again.

We don't need experts to tell us what the basic message of the Bible means. But we do need them to help us see the nuances, the subtleties, and the fine points. We can avail ourselves of their assistance through their books and through Bible studies that employ good scholarship. Some scholars write for the laity. Others study the scholarly publications and digest them for us. A number of excellent "study Bibles" are annotated by professional biblical studies teachers with decades of experience in interpreting the Bible. Especially commendable are *The HarperCollins Study Bible* and *The New Oxford Annotated Bible,* both of which use the NRSV. Using the guides provided by these scholars, we can recover a great deal of what is lost in translation.

Furthermore, whatever translation we may choose, there are ways of compensating for the detriment of translations. It is always important to compare our translation with others. I have found it helpful to have members of a Bible study group read different translations. That usually facilitates discussion of the differences and helps participants come to a better understanding of passages. In comparing translations, we find some of what may be lost in any one particular translation.

Surely the most important means of finding that which is lost in translation is to study the Bible with other Christians under competent guidance (such guidance may be a person or a good study program). In groups we can seek new understanding of the Bible that takes us beyond the restrictions of translations. We can find meaning for our lives in the Bible.

Chapter Five ————————————
How Can I Find Meaning in the Bible?

Devout Christians sometimes complain that they simply do not find reading the Bible helpful. They seek meaning for their lives in the Bible but are disappointed not to find it there. I have had that same experience. On many Sunday mornings I have come to worship with a nagging sense of meaninglessness, looking for direction. The Scripture lessons, however, have often seemed pointless, at least so far as my quest for meaning was concerned. I remember one occasion when I seemed adrift in my profession and yearned for my niche in the church's ministry. The psalm we chanted that Sunday claimed that God rewards the righteous with prosperity and happiness. It simply did not fit my experience at the time and seemed even to assert something that was not true.

Meaning for life is elusive. It is even hard to explain what we mean by meaning and meaninglessness. What we often seek, however, is a purpose for life that reaches into every corner of our experience. What is our reason for being? Why were we born? We need purpose that soaks into our pours, saturates our personalities, and colors our world in shades of hope and possibility.

Is it reasonable to suppose that Bible reading and study help to supply us with that kind of meaning and purpose? The church has persistently claimed it is. Chapter 2 argued that the Bible's central message has to do with God's efforts to establish a relationship with us. In that relationship with our Creator, life becomes fresh, bringing in a new quality of living. However you may define salvation, surely it has to do with a perspective on life and the world that transforms both into meaningful realities.

How then do we learn to read and study the Bible in ways that facilitate our discovery of meaning? What is entailed in reading Scripture to find meaning for our lives? This chapter treats this issue and proposes a method of studying a biblical passage. It is a "how to" chapter in which I will suggest a procedure for meaningful Bible reading. The procedure may not work as well for you as it does for me, and you may need to make some adjustments to it. Try it and then make your own modifications to fit your reading style.

Preparation for Reading

We want to find meaning for our lives through reading the Bible. If we are to succeed, we need to ready ourselves for reading. The preparation entails a heightened sense of self-awareness. This means being acutely conscious of who you are and what your feeling or mood is at the moment. Part of the sense of who we are at any moment entails our sensitivity to God's presence. I may feel entirely alienated from God. Or, I may have a heightened trust in God's presence in the Spirit. Knowing the state of your faith is part of the acute consciousness we need as we prepare for Bible study. If we are preparing for private Bible reading, we should take time to reflect on our lives at that moment. If we are in a group preparing for Bible study, we should share with one another how we are feeling about life right now. Each individual may be in a different place in faith's journey. Talk about that.

We never read the Bible in a vacuum. We always read it as people engaged with the world and all the joys and sorrows that involves. We read the Bible as a community of faith engaged in much the same way. There may be common problems, pressing issues, and deep concerns. The purpose of an exercise for preparation for reading (whether individually or in a group) is to bring our experience with us to the biblical text. We dredge the feelings and moods out of the recesses of our lives and put them on the table alongside the Bible. To fail to do this means that we may not be open to hear what God might want to say to us through Scripture. Consciousness of our particular feelings at the moment may also help us avoid reading something into a text that is not really there.

This introspection, whether individual or communal, is groundwork for meaningful Bible study. Once we have done the groundwork, we are ready to focus attention on the passage we are reading and studying. The shift from self to Bible is a drastic one. But as we glue ourselves to the text, our self and group consciousness is never lost. They are just taking a role in the background.

Step One: First Reading

The first task is to limit the passage you want to read. Try to isolate a segment that deals with one issue. Trying to read large chunks of Scripture at a time usually means that we do not do justice to the whole of it. Ten or twelve verses is usually enough. However, look for "markers" in the text that indicate the beginning of a new topic or story. Begin there and read until you come to another such indication that a particular story or episode has ended or that the conversation has moved to another topic. Sometimes the subheads used in modern translations will help you decide what constitutes a block of text.

We cannot assign too much importance to chapter and verse divisions. Such divisions crept into the biblical documents rather late in the process of their copying. In some cases, a chapter break indicates a change of thought or a shift in the story being told. But they are rather arbitrary in many instances.

Genesis 1:1—2:4a, for instance, constitutes a single story of God's creation. When you notice that 2:5 reads, "No plant of the field was yet in the earth," you realize that a new story begins in the middle of verse 4. The second story in 2:4b-25 is connected with the first but comprises another account of creation.

Limit the passage you want to read. These are some examples of what might be appropriate passages in terms of their length: Genesis 15:1-6, Psalm 8, Amos 5:18-34, Matthew 22:15-22, and 1 Corinthians 1:10-17.

Now take note of the context in which you find your passage. Remember the old adage in buying a house: three things are important—location, location, location. The location of a biblical passage is equally important. Before reading a selected portion, skim what comes just before the passage. In this first reading, continue beyond the passage itself into what follows it. Get acquainted with the passage's neighbors on either side (before and after it). What is the preceding episode in a story? What issues are discussed before and after your passage?

We have a place to begin and a place to stop, and we are equipped with a sense of what precedes and follows the passage. Now read the passage through carefully but continuously from beginning to end. Get a general idea of what it is about. Mark something to which you want to return but don't stop now to consider it. You want to gain a general impression of the passage and what's going on in it before continuing to the next step.

Step Two: Understanding the Form and Parts

Having gained a general impression of the whole of the passage and its context, there are two questions you should try to answer in this second step: What is the literary form of the passage? What parts make up the passage?

Literary Form of the Passage

Determining the literary form of a passage is not as hard as it may sound. Are you reading a story? Does the passage speak of events that happened in an order—one occurring then and another at another time? Or, is it poetry? Unlike the old manuscripts, in English translations poetic passages will be presented in poetic form, different from prose. (There are some advantages to reading a translation.) Or, is the passage an argument of some sort? Perhaps the author is trying to prove that something is true or trying to convince readers to act in a certain way. Perhaps the passage is a segment of God's commands for the people.

You might want to consider the following examples to help you identify other forms: Genesis 1:1—2:4a is story. Notice it has a chronological sequence—what God did in each of seven days. Exodus 14 tells the story of Israel's crossing of the Red Sea and how their Egyptian pursuers were drowned. It is a narrative tale telling of a series of events. But in Exodus 15, the literary form changes. "The Song of Moses" is poetry. Much of Deuteronomy (4:44—28:68) is comprised of a series of commandments or instructions concerning justice. Deuteronomy 22:22-30 contains a series of such instructions. Here you are reading legal material in the form of case studies (if such and such a situation should exist, do so and so). Proverbs 3:13-18 is a collection of wise sayings that guide moral behavior.

As I have already mentioned, what kind of literature the passage is determines how we read it. We read novels differently than we read history books, science fiction differently than news magazines, and newspapers differently than collections of poems. The Bible contains a variety of literary forms, so we need to be alert to the kind of writing we are reading. Poetry will, for instance, be filled with images—word pictures—that provoke our imaginations. Exodus 15:8 says, "At the blast of your [God's] nostrils the waters piled up." It is a metaphor, saying God caused the division of the water so Israel could pass over to the other side.

In summary, some of the major forms we encounter in the Bible include story, poetry, law, and moral exhortation. Other forms of which you may need to be conscious are letters (like Paul's epistles), wise sayings (for example, the book of Proverbs), prophetic declarations (see Isaiah), written pieces to be used in worship (for example, Psalm 15), hymns (such as Philippians 2:5-11), and creeds (like Romans 1:2-4). Another form is the apocalyptic literature to which I referred earlier. The word *apocalyptic* is the English version of a Greek word that means unveiling or revealing. So the title of the last book of the Bible is The Revelation to John. Another example of this form is found in chapter 13 of Mark.

Apocalyptic literature has a form of its own, although it may incorporate the other forms listed here. For example, Revelation as a whole is an apocalyptic form, but within it we find passages that contain what appear to be portions of liturgy intended for worship (see 15:3-4 for an example).

Determining the literary form of the passage helps prepare us to understand it. We don't look for the same kind of logic in poetry as we do in a reading of Paul or the legal sections of Deuteronomy. Sometimes, of course, we will need to make sure we correctly understand a particular kind of literature. Prophetic literature and legend are occasions when that may be necessary.

Prophecy in English has come to mean "predicting the future." But that definition does not work in the Bible. Biblical prophetic literature is the proclamation of God's will. So, when the prophets of the Old Testament challenge the people, they are declaring God's will for them. That may be condemnation of their sins. The prophet may speak of the consequences of those sins. But the prophet's message may also be words of assurance and promise.

Many of the stories in the Old Testament are legendary. That does not mean they have no historical basis. It means they contain historical fact and fictional embellishments. We have already suggested that something like this happened in the stories about Israel's release from slavery in Egypt and their occupation of the land of Canaan. Elijah, too, was a kind of larger-than-life-prophet. He was so revered that the story in 2 Kings 2 claims he never died. He was taken into heaven in a whirlwind. We read such stories with acknowledgment that they have some roots in history but understand they also appeal to the imagination.

Parts of the Passage

With a basic understanding of the passage's literary form, now look at the whole of it and determine what its parts are. Identify the components that come together to form the passage.

In Paul's argument for the resurrection of the body in 1 Corinthians 15:12-34, we detect stages in his discussion. Notice that he begins by asking the question he thinks readers are asking by this time (verse 12). He argues first that the believer's resurrection is a logical result of Christ's resurrection (verses 13-16). If that result is not true, then our faith is without any hope (verses 17-19). Then he moves into a comparison of the accomplishments of Adam and Christ (verses 20-22). Next he describes the "order" of events before Christians are raised (verses 23-28). The argument takes an abrupt turn in verse 29: "You baptize on behalf of the dead. Why would you do that if there were no resurrection of the dead?" The last verses are a personal argument. Paul and others suffer in this life. If there were no resurrection, we should all "eat, drink, and be merry." But instead we live moral lives because the dead are raised (verses 30-34). Notice how verse 35 raises another question. "But someone will ask, 'How are the dead raised? With what kind of body do they come?'" Now Paul shifts his argument to the kind of bodies we will be given in the resurrection (verses 35-49).

Another example shows how different building blocks make up Psalm 23. The first three verses are a declaration of God's role as a shepherd and what God does in that role. In verses 4-5 the psalmist next imagines the loneliest and most fearful of situations—"the valley of the shadow of death." God is present even in those situations. Even in the presence of enemies, God cares for us. The final verse is a statement of confidence in the future. Believers are sure of God's "goodness and mercy" and dwell with God for their whole lives. The psalm demonstrates a clear progression through each of these three reflective steps.

A story is no different from these two examples, except that the parts of a story are individual events. I will discuss the division of the story in Mark 5:24b-34 in Step Three below. In a story the plot moves along by things that happen.

Identifying the parts that make up a passage helps us understand how it works. How does Paul's argument for resurrection try to convince the reader? How does Psalm 23 make an effective affirmation of faith? We do not understand the way a passage affects us until we can discern the steps through which it takes us. How, for instance, do the individual parts of the story of Jesus' crucifixion in Mark 15:21-41 function together to make this such a powerful story? In identifying a passage's individual parts, we create a kind of map for our reading. We know the route the passage will take us.

We have identified the literary form of our passage and its individual parts. We can now investigate its details.

Step Three: A Close Reading

A close reading is simply a careful word-by-word detailed consideration of the passage. It proceeds in a conversational way. Readers ask questions of the text and then look for how it addresses each question. Think of this process like getting acquainted with a person you do not know. You ask the person questions about her- or himself. Where are you from? What are your interests? The actual questions we use to become acquainted with a biblical passage may need to vary according to the literary form of the text (for instance, whether it is a story or an argument). But the questions suggested below will generally work to open the text's meaning for us.

We will use Mark 5:24b-34 as an example of how a close reading works. Assume that in the first two steps we have already determined that this passage is a story. In terms of its context, it is an episode in Jesus' ministry sandwiched between two parts of another story—the healing of Jairus' daughter (5:21-24a and 35-43). The healing of the woman with the flow of blood has these parts: a setting for the story (verse 24b), a description of the woman's condition (verses 25-26), her healing by touching Jesus' garment (verses 27-29), Jesus' effort to identify who touched him (verses 30-32), the woman's confession that she is the one (verses 33), and Jesus' words to her (verse 34). We are ready now for a close reading of the story and ask three questions of it.

Where Does the Passage Reach a Climax?

Nearly every passage comes to a climax. (There may be some that leave us hanging, like Mark 16:1-8.) The climax is most often in the conclusion or what immediately precedes the conclusion. But the climactic point of a passage can be most anywhere. Readers must use their judgment of where the passage seems to say most clearly and precisely what it is attempting to communicate.

In the case of the woman with the flow of blood, the climax is in Jesus' words to the woman in verse 34: "Daughter, your faith has made you well; go in peace, and be healed of your disease." The woman has already been healed of her ailment in verse 29. But in this case that is not the climax. Jesus' words mean something more than physical healing. *Well* implies a wholeness that entails her faith—the faith that brought her to Jesus (see verse 28)—as well as her bodily health. *Daughter* claims her as a member of Jesus' family with God. *Peace* suggests a new kind of life as a member of that family.

Since we ask about the passage's climax at the beginning of our close reading, we may have to revise our initial sense of where that apex is. As we study the passage in more detail, we may find that the climactic point was elsewhere than we first thought. But we answer this question tentatively and proceed with the other questions to see whether or not our first impression was correct.

What Words Are Prominent?

Words may achieve prominence by being repeated several times. But sometimes they gain their prominence by their position in the passage. What words, for instance, gain prominence by their place in the climax of the passage?

Prominent words are clues to a passage's major emphasis and message. In the story of Jesus' healing, for instance, the word *daughter* stands out, not because it is repeated, but because it recasts the entire story. So it has a surprising prominence. *Healed* and *well* are two other prominent words. The woman expresses her faith in being made well by touching Jesus' garment (verse 28). In the next verse she is healed. And both *healed* and *well* are used in the story's climax (verse 34). The prominence of these words is implied by their absence in verse 26. The medical profession has not supplied her healing or wellness.

But another word stands out in the story by virtue of its repetition: *touch* (verses 27, 28, 30, and 31). All the woman had to do was touch Jesus' garment. Notice too that, in this case, it is she who touches him. The story is different from those in which Jesus touches others to heal them (for example, Mark 1:40-42).

What Details Seem Important?

Details are often more important than general impressions. The meaning of a passage may be hidden away in the small features or seemingly incidental words. It is like the fine points of needlework. Sometimes in our concern to identify the general thrust of a biblical passage we ignore the details. Or, we try to read too fast, and the specifics elude us. In our contemporary culture there is a good deal of pressure on us to read quickly. Time is precious, so we must read and digest information quickly. Newspapers are written so that articles can be skimmed, and the substance of an article is nearly always in the first short paragraph. In the case of the Bible, fast reading does not make for meaningful reading. A close reading pays attention to the fine points of a passage.

In the story of Jesus' healing of the woman in Mark 5, the details are illuminating. We notice, for instance, a number of details: This woman has suffered for "twelve years" (verse 25). She came up to Jesus from "behind" (verse 27). Her speech is never quoted except when she speaks to herself in verse 28. She finally comes face to face with Jesus in "fear and trembling." She "fell" before Jesus and "told him the whole truth" (verse 33). We have already marked the details of Jesus' words to her in the climax of the passage.

The details of this story tell us a good deal about this woman. She is reluctant to bother Jesus with her problem, especially in the crowd. She only touches his garment, never speaking to him directly. She is awed by his person and afraid of what he might do or say as a result of her touching his clothing. But she is willing to confess the whole thing, lying there at his feet.

When we look at the details of a passage, we may be surprised by all that we learn. Biblical writers often tell us very little about characters' inner feelings or personalities. But in the small acts attributed to them, biblical passages often communicate a good deal. The words of the psalm, for instance, frequently express a feeling toward oppressors, even though the inner feeling may not be named in so many words (for instance, Psalm 22:12-13). Meaning is often in the details.

In a close reading, we ask the text questions. But it may also raise other questions for us, some of which we cannot answer. When those questions seem important, seek some help. Read the notes in your study Bible, look up some words in a Bible dictionary, and consult a commentary. (See Suggestions for Further Reading at the end of this book.)

Step Four: The Meaning for My Life

After we have completed a close reading of the passage, we are ready to reflect on its whole meaning. Now our preliminary work begins to pay off. We might proceed through this final step in three stages. The first stage keeps the focus on the passage, and the second stage brings it closer to us and our experience. The third stage entails how we appropriate meaning from the text.

What Is a General Meaning of the Passage?

First we need to try to summarize the meaning of the passage as a whole. But let's be realistic about what we can accomplish at this point. We cannot claim to capture the whole meaning of a passage. Nor can we pretend that we understand precisely what the author intended to say in it. All we hope to achieve is one of the text's possible meanings. Others may find different meanings. That is good and proper. Any biblical text is rich enough to yield different meanings at different times for different people. It is like a good piece of poetry. You discuss it with others, but no one pretends to have exhausted all the nuances of a Shakespearean sonnet. Neither do we pretend to exhaust the possible meaning of our biblical passage with our puny summary of it.

To be sure, not just any old meaning can be claimed as arising from a biblical passage. What we seek is a statement of the sense of the passage for us at a certain time. What we say a passage means must be supported by the passage itself—what it actually says and how it says it. So, the passage puts boundaries on what we can claim it means. If someone argues the story of the healing of the woman in Mark 5 means that women are inferior, that they should be inconspicuous and silent, we ask how that statement could possibly be harmonized with Jesus' words to her in the story's climax.

What we attempt to do is identify a possible meaning the passage has on the basis of what we now know about it. We should try to state that meaning in a concise sentence. This is another place where group Bible study is more productive than private study. In a group, we are called to tell others as clearly and precisely as we can what we think a passage means for us. Others then respond with their statements and perhaps lead us to see what we had not discerned. In private biblical study, I find it helpful to try to write a few words about the meaning of a passage as I am able to identify it. Writing this forces me to become specific and precise.

On the basis of our study of Mark 5:24b-34 we might write, "Jesus values faith that arises from humility and modesty." Humility and modesty attempt to summarize the woman's behavior. Jesus' valuing her faith seeks to capture the essence of his commendation of the woman. Faith describes both what the woman hoped for in touching Jesus' garment and what Jesus himself ascribes to her.

With Whom (or What) Do You Identify in the Passage?

At this point we begin to bring ourselves more consciously into the process. Our "selves" and our experience have been in the background all the time we have been working with the passage. Now we locate a bridge between us and the text. That bridge is often (although perhaps not always) found in identification. Identification is the recognition that we see ourselves—or some part of ourselves—in the passage. Have you sometimes seen yourself in a television character? Does a character appeal to you because she or he is like you in some way? I confess I identify with Tim, "the Toolman," Taylor on *Home Improvement*. Like him, I love motors and machinery, but—also like him—I am unbelievably inept when it comes to mechanical things.

Reading biblical passages we often find ourselves in the text through identification. A character in a story may behave the way we have behaved or wanted to behave. Sometimes we identify with the villain in the biblical story. I see myself in Nicodemus, in his dullness and blindness brought on by his assumptions that he knows how God works (John 3:1-16). Sometimes I identify with Elijah in his depression (1 Kings 19:1-10). Sometimes it is better to look for ourselves in the villains than in the heroes and in negative as well as positive features of a character.

But sometimes we identify, too, with words and not characters. The words of a psalm, for instance, may express what we have said or wanted to say. A command may seem to have been written just for us. Words of consolation may sound like they were intended for our feelings. Identification, therefore, is broader than personalities. It includes the sensation that words fit us as if a tailor had created them just for us.

Broadly understood, identification is our entryway into a passage—a viaduct from our situation, across the gulf, and into the Bible. Through identification we "read ourselves" into biblical texts. We become a character or characters in the story. We become the recipient of the words, a listener sitting in the corner of the house in which Paul is preaching or on the edge of the crowd to which Amos speaks. Through identification we leave our chairs and walk onto the stage to become participants in the biblical drama.

What fits you like a tailored garment in the story of the healing of that woman in Mark 5? It might be the woman herself, the disciples who cannot understand Jesus' effort to identify the one who touched him, or even Jesus himself stressed by the crowd and their demands on his time.

I find something of myself in this woman in Mark 5, especially on those occasions when I am not feeling good about myself and am wrestling with self-doubt and inadequacy. This happened to me while preparing a sermon on Mark 5:24-34. I watched this woman approach Jesus from behind to touch his garment (verse 27). I knew the feelings she must have had. I felt that I was not worthy to approach Jesus directly. She helped me identify and drew me into the text. Then Jesus' words to the woman became words addressed to me, as if he was saying, "Bob . . ." Jesus' words healed the woman. Jesus calls her "daughter" (verse 34). Even in my unworthy state, I too could approach Jesus from behind, and he would affirm that I am a "son." The passage seemed to be written for me at that very moment.

What Is the Passage's Meaning for Me?

Identification already clarifies the meaning a passage has for us and our lives. When we cross the gulf between ourselves and our experience into the midst of the passage, it wraps us in its meaning. But further reflection is needed. Once we seem to have a handle on the text's message for us, we don't stop there. The moment is too powerful for that. We have to ask what this meaning means.

One meaning is Scripture's ability to change within us something about the way we are going to live. We are responsible for thinking that through. Meaning usually becomes real for us only when we can live it. Meaning that makes us feel or think something can slip away as quickly as it came. But if we can live it for a time, translate it into action, then it becomes a part of us.

The Gospel of John begins by calling Christ the Word. The Greek noun translated "Word" in John 1:1-18 is *logos*. One definition of *logos* in Greek philosophy of the time was "meaning." Interestingly, this passage goes on to say in verse 14 that "the Word (*logos*) became flesh and lived among us." The meaning became "fleshed out" in a human being who lived that meaning. At the core of our Christian faith is the idea that life's meaning must be lived out just as Christ lived out God's love. Consequently, a text's meaning for our lives must first be lived before we can really claim it as our own. By living meaning, we appropriate it.

Reflect on the meaning the passage has for you. Then decide on a response by which you can—in some way—live that meaning. When possible, we should identify something we can do, actions we can take as a result of the text's meaning. But be realistic. Decide to act at least once in a way that embodies the meaning. It does not have to be an ambitious project (feeding the hungry people of the world, for example), but it should be concrete.

Because of the meaning I found in Mark 5:24b-34, I will remember that Christ has declared I am a child of God. When I am tempted toward depression and self-doubt, I will remember this declaration of my identity. To help me remember, I will use the sign of the cross as a means of recalling my baptism. This is a concrete act, a physical embodiment of the message I found in this story. I am a child of God. In some similar way, I urge you to take ownership of the meaning you find in Scripture.

Reviewing the Process

As a guide for your Bible reading, what follows outlines the steps of the reading process:

Preparation for Reading
>   Be conscious of who you are and what your situation is.

Step One: First Reading
>   Limit the portion you will read.
>   Determine the context of the passage.
>   Read it through once from beginning to end.

Step Two: Understanding Forms and Parts
    What is the literary form of the passage?
    What parts make up the passage?

Step Three: A Close Reading
    Where does the passage reach a climax?
    What words are prominent?
    What details are important?

Step Four: The Meaning for My Life
    What is the general meaning of the passage?
    With whom (or what) do I identify in the passage?
    What is the meaning of the passage for me?

There are two principles of this process, and they are really quite simple. The first is to pay close attention to the passage itself, its form, parts, words, and details. The second principle involves the relationship between the reader's experience and the passage. Notice that you were asked to begin with a consciousness of yourself and your situation. At the conclusion of the process, you were invited to return to yourself and your experience.

Finding meaning for your life in the Bible really entails discovering the connection between its message and your experience. Within that process of discovering the connection, I believe God speaks through Scripture to our situation. For that, we will want to give God thanks.But there are some biblical passages that seem to have no connection with our lives. What are we to do with them?

Chapter Six ————————————
What Are We to Make of the Old Testament?

"DAVID ... KILLED EIGHTEEN THOUSAND EDOMITES in the Valley of Salt.... And the Lord gave victory to David wherever he went" (2 Samuel 8:13-14). One does not have to be a pacifist Christian to wonder about a passage such as this. And this passage is but one among many in which God is said to have sanctioned and even commanded violence and slaughter.

The Old Testament has disturbed a good many Christians. As early as the second century, an influential Christian named Marcion disowned the Old Testament. He believed and taught others that the God of the Old Testament was a different god from God "the Father" whom Jesus revealed. But the church resisted those teachings. It labeled Marcion a "heretic" and continued to affirm the Hebrew Scriptures as its canon. The problem of the first Testament of the Bible is not a new one. It is not just a modern sensitivity that is sometimes offended by portions of this part of our Bible.

Many today appreciate Marcion's efforts. What are we to make of the fact that the first Testament seems so frequently to be at odds with the God we believe is revealed in Jesus of Nazareth? How do we find meaning for our lives from Scripture that pictures God in such a way?

The issue, of course, is complicated. This chapter will try to unravel the complications and identify the ways in which the first Testament of our Bible is rich with possibilities of meaning for our lives. Three basic questions provide us a way through this process: What is the nature of some Old Testament literature? How should we understand the cultures out of which that literature came? And how can we appreciate its teachings?

One caution: The Old Testament is large and varied. Consequently, we must be careful in making sweeping statements about it. (That, incidentally, was Marcion's mistake.)

What Is Special about Old Testament Literature?

The writings of the Old Testament arose over a period of nearly two thousand years. The actual writing of the documents may not have begun in the first half of that period. The nature of those documents is our first concern.

The Folk Literature of the Old Testament

Some of the Old Testament documents record stories and teachings preserved over decades in oral form. They were remembered and told over and over, and passed on to each new generation. They were stories and teachings that conserved the people's history and defined their identity. They were told around the campfire, celebrated on certain important occasions, and treasured in the people's collective memory.

Much of the Old Testament is like what we would call folk literature. It is the literature of the common people and deals with their basic understanding of themselves and the world. As we noted in the last chapter, history and legend appear to be woven together in many of these stories. In these cases, some basic historical facts look like they have been embellished to strengthen the story. We have our own folk literature. Every Thanksgiving Day we retell the story of the pilgrims' dinner with the Powhatan. And that story—whatever its historical basis may be—has been elaborated through imagination. But we cherish it because it helps us remember our roots and creates a foundation for our basic identity as North Americans. The literature of the Old Testament is often similar.

The book of Genesis is a good example. It retells the stories that led to the creation of the people of Israel—those twelve tribes that eventually settled in Canaan. The Genesis stories proceed in four stages. The first stage is creation and the earliest history of humanity (chapters 1–11). Scholars call this "primordial history" because it probes the mysterious origins of humanity. For instance, the story of the tower of Babel (11:1-9) explains how humans were scattered around the world and came to speak different languages. The explanation is not scientific, but legendary. The story is rooted in something that is fundamental to humans, namely pride and an ambition to reach up into heaven and dwell with God.

The next three stages of the Genesis story move closer to the Hebrew people. The stories of Abraham and Sarah establish the people's origins (12:1—25:18). The Jacob stories (25:19—36:43) and those of Joseph (chapters 37–50) trace the earliest family events and conclude with the Israelites living in Egypt. Do you have stories in your family history about some ancestor and what she or he did? How about stories of how your family came to dwell in a particular place?

Understanding this kind of Old Testament literature helps us appreciate the nature of some these stories and the various cultures in which they were preserved.

Where Did It Come From?

Folk literature is often concerned with the question of where something or someone came from. How did some practice originate? The question of how some practice originated is often addressed in folk literature. The example of the tower of Babel above is one such story. Our own national, ethnic, and family stories do the same kind of thing. We celebrate the Fourth of July to recall the birth and independence of our nation. Lincoln's journey from a log cabin in Illinois to the presidency reinforces our belief that all people have a chance to succeed in the United States. People cherish stories that explain why things are the way they are.

Not surprisingly, Old Testament literature has similar stories. Some explain why humans are the way they are. A strange story in Genesis 6:4 explains the existence of legendary warrior heroes called "Nephilim." They were the offspring of sexual unions between angelic beings ("sons of God") and human women. Extraordinary humans were the blending of the divine and human.

Genesis 3 is basically a statement about why humans no longer live in a paradise but suffer separate from God. The creation of Eve out of a rib taken from Adam in Genesis 2:21-24 tries to account for why men are attracted to women. It also suggests why the male warrior is vulnerable below the rib cage.

Yet, these stories are fundamentally religious. They offer an explanation of God and the human relationship with God.

Some of the stories that seek to explain where things come from focus on specific religious practices. The question of circumcision was important. Circumcision came to represent the uniqueness of Hebraic identity. The Hebrews had to explain this practice to their children, as well as to people of other nations and cultures. So stories offer such explanations. The commandment to circumcise male children is rooted in the covenant God made with Abraham, Sarah, and their descendants. Circumcision was "a sign of the covenant" between God and the people (Genesis 17:11-14). Its importance shows up in the strange and puzzling story about God's effort to kill Moses (or his son—the words are not clear) in Exodus 4:24-26. Zipporah, Moses' wife, circumcises their son and calls Moses "a bridegroom of blood by circumcision." This story suggests shedding blood represented Israel's commitment to God and provides protection against deadly forces.

As strange as this story is, it foreshadows the use of blood in Israel's escape from slavery in Egypt and the establishment of Passover (Exodus 12). That celebration and the practice of eating unleavened bread is explained in the final plague God is said to have inflicted in order to win the people's freedom (Exodus 12:1—13:16).

Other stories have to do with the origin and practice of the Sabbath rest. The regulation, of course, is among the ten commandments in Exodus 20:8-11. In Deuteronomy 5:12-15, Israel's release from slavery in Egypt is symbolized in the Sabbath (5:15). The Exodus passage appeals to the tradition that God created the world in six days and rested on the seventh (Genesis 2:2). The difference between the two explanations for keeping the Sabbath may suggest that different Hebraic communities treasured different reasons for the practice, or that the reasons changed over a period of time.

These examples are enough to suggest the role of some of the early stories in the Old Testament. But another dimension of nearly all the stories and teachings of the Old Testament helps us even more.

The World of the Old Testament Stories

A story of any kind creates its own peculiar world. Readers gain an impression of a world—a particular environment—through the way a story is told, what events are narrated, and what the story takes for granted. Think of the popular stories the Walt Disney Corporation has produced as movies. Those imaginative stories create peculiar worlds. In the Disney interpretation of *Beauty and the Beast,* a teapot and cups and saucers sing and dance. In *The Hunchback of Notre Dame,* the gargoyles speak. These motion pictures invite viewers into particular kinds of worlds and ask them to believe those worlds for a time. Science fiction stories do the same thing. The *Star Wars* films create their own narrative world. The same is true of biographies of famous people. The story-teller tries to fashion a narrative world in which readers can come closer to the experience of the featured subject or subjects. Narrative worlds have little to do with what is true and what is fantasy. The telling of both history and fantasy entails a world in which the story is told.

The Old Testament stories create a distinctive world into which readers are invited. The environments of the stories have distinct features that are different from the world that you and I inhabit on a daily basis.

First, the whole of the biblical world is open. We live in a world that, for the most part, is closed. We assume that natural laws control our world. If I throw my pen into the air, it will come down. The law of gravity is at work. The sun sets at the end of each day and rises again the next morning. Our planet revolves around the sun and produces the regularity of the days and nights. Our world is tightly controlled by natural law.

The biblical world (including the New Testament world), on the other hand, does not assume such predictability. There was little conception of natural law as such, certainly not any absolute law that was seldom, if ever, violated. The world was open. Anything could happen anytime. To be sure, God established a certain regularity in nature. But that regularity was open to variation (for example, Joshua 10:13). Consequently, the biblical world is one in which anything is possible. God was in direct control of the world and events in the world. God was free to act as the divine will chose. To some degree or another, most modern people have put a body of regulations between the world and God. God governs the world through these regulations. In the Bible's world, God is busy every moment directly running the affairs of nature.

Healing, for instance, is common in the biblical world, since there were no hard and fast medical laws to govern health (for instance, 2 Kings 5:1-19). Furthermore, God frequently uses what we would call natural phenomena to accomplish the divine will. God's angel afflicts Judah's enemy (the Assyrians) with a plague, and their king must turn back without conquering Jerusalem (2 Kings 19:35-36). Political events are also occasions for God's direct actions in the world. The defeats and exiles of Israel and Judah result from God's punishment of them for their sin (for example, Jeremiah 18:13-17). But later the defeat of Judah's enemy, the Babylonians, the rise of a new kingdom, and the edict allowing the people to return to their homeland are also God's doing (for example, Isaiah 45:1-4 and 49:8-12). The biblical world was open to all these possibilities.

The second feature of the Bible's story world (especially the Old Testament) arises from the first: God is everywhere present and active. God pops up again and again as a character in these stories. God speaks, gets angry, repents, acts, and grieves. One of the difficult features of the stories in the Old Testament is the image of God they suggest. Most of us know God through faith, through the words and actions of other people, through intuitive kinds of knowing, and through the sacraments. But the Old Testament characters encounter God directly. God comes "out of the blue" to speak personally with them. Abraham, Moses, Jeremiah, and others all have conversations with God. The stories often ask us to suspend our disbelief, to believe such direct conversations with God are possible.

But we are also startled by how human the Old Testament often seems to make God. Some stories make God into another human character with many of the same characteristics we have. Several of the divine characteristics in the Old Testament may offend some Christians today. God is "jealous" (for example, Exodus 34:14). But God's jealousy was a way of expressing how committed God was to Israel. How else do we say that? Moreover, God gets angry and acts violently, just as we are prone to do. First Kings 11:9-13 declares that God became angry with Solomon and tore the kingdom from him and his descendants. The results are told in 1 Kings 12. After Solomon's death, the kingdom is divided between the north and the south.

Of course, divine anger is not limited to the Old Testament. The New Testament suggests that God's anger at the religious establishment in Jerusalem results in the city's destruction (for example, Luke 21:20-24). The New Testament writers clearly thought the Roman defeat of the Jewish revolt (c.e. 66 to 70) was God's punishment of the people's sin. Moreover, the book of Revelation is filled with God's violent destruction of evil (for example, read Revelation 20:7-10).

The picture of God as a human character results from several things. Most important of all, humans have no other way to speak of God except in terms of who we are. Even though we may not speak of God in such extreme human ways (for example, changing one's mind), we still attribute human characteristics to God. We say that God loves, shows mercy, forgives, speaks through the Bible, hears our prayers, and cares about human suffering. But how else can one speak of a God who is beyond language? The Old Testament simply does so in full honesty and openness.

But assigning God such human characteristics also makes for wonderfully exciting stories. The Old Testament stories are exhilarating because, in them, humans are dealing with a God who has the full range of human attributes. So, when in Exodus 32 God appears and is angry, Moses can plead with the Lord not to punish the people. For a time we readers are held in suspense, wondering what God will do. We are relieved when, at verse 14, we learn that God "changed his mind about the disaster that he planned to bring on his people."

This is not to say that God gets twisted into a human character for the sake of a good story. But in folk literature it makes for good and adventuresome story-telling. We will never know how literally the Hebrew people took these stories. They did not make a sharp distinction between pure history and imaginative telling of history. Our conception of history as an accurate representation of the facts is a modern invention (and, incidentally, one that contemporary historians entirely disavow). The biblical writers and first readers did not make the sharp distinction we do between fact and imagination. Some truth had to be understood and expressed in imaginative pictures. That was the only way it could be comprehended. We can understand this experience. Poetry, we say, can express some truth that scientific description cannot. How else shall I express how much I love my wife except in poetic picture language?

This effort to understand the story world of the Old Testament neither entirely solves our problems with it, nor does it completely ease our discomfort with the image of God in it. But perhaps it allows us to read the first Testament with a bit more appreciation and readiness to hear its message. But the literary character of the Old Testament's stories is entangled in the matter of culture.

How Did Culture Influence the Old Testament?

The importance of culture has been mentioned frequently in this book. The Bible is a product of a number of different cultures. Those cultures determined not only the language in which the contents of the Bible were written. They also influenced the contents themselves. Humans always think and understand within their culture. Cultural values shape how we think, how we understand, and what we regard as important.

Cultural Variety in the Old Testament

Therefore, we ought not to be surprised that the Old Testament is a cultural statement. Its writers, too, worked within a cultural environment. They were human and could do no other. Whatever inspiration led them, those responsible for the Old Testament experienced it within a cultural context. To understand any part of the Old Testament we must understand the culture out of which it came.

The Old Testament stories arose, were preserved, and finally written in a number of different cultural settings. Over a long period of nearly two thousand years, the Hebrew people developed and lived in different societies. These societies were culturally different from each other.

One of the easiest cultural differences to detect is the contrast between the nomadic and agricultural settings. Some Old Testament passages, for instance those in Numbers, preserve the period when the people lived a wandering life. They moved from place to place to find sufficient pasture land for their livestock. Deuteronomy 26:5 incorporates this period in a basic Hebraic confession of faith: "A wandering Aramean was my ancestor"— a likely reference to Abraham. In Deuteronomy itself, however, many of the commands of God suppose that the people are farmers settled in one place and making their livelihood off the land. Read, for instance, Deuteronomy 23:24-25. It allows picking grapes and grain from your neighbors' fields as long as you do not do so in excess.

Cultural Influences on the Old Testament

Some examples may help us appreciate the way different cultures influenced the Old Testament. The first example results from the fact that 1 and 2 Chronicles give us another and later version of the materials we find in 1 and 2 Samuel and 1 and 2 Kings. The books of Samuel and Kings are part of a larger history that scholars believe took its initial form in the middle of the sixth century, B.C.E. The books of Chronicles were written two hundred years later, after the people have returned from exile and resettled in Judah.

A vivid difference between 1 Chronicles and 2 Samuel appears in their respective accounts of David's decision to take a census of the people. The census was probably for the purpose of forcing men to serve in the army. Second Samuel 24:1 reads: "Again the anger of the Lord was kindled against Israel, and he incited David against them, saying, 'Go, count the people of Israel and Judah.'" When 1 Chronicles tells that same story, it begins with these words: "Satan stood up against Israel and incited David to count the people of Israel" (1 Chronicles 21:1).

In 2 Samuel, God inspires David to do an evil deed then punishes David and Israel for the sin (2 Samuel 24:10-17). The chronicler attributes the evil inspiration to Satan.

We may find the story in Chronicles more appealing. It is difficult for some of us to understand how God inspires an evil deed and then punishes the people for it. The story in 2 Samuel assumes that God is responsible for all inspiration, whether it be for good or for evil. The image of God in this story took shape in an earlier cultural setting when the Hebrews believed God was the only force there was. The mighty Lord was free to contrive situations to accomplish the divine will.

But the chronicler lived in another time and culture. By then the Jewish people recognized the existence of an evil force that inspired deeds opposing God's will. The concept of Satan as an opponent to God took shape in the two hundred or so years between the two accounts. During those intervening years, the people experienced the exile from their homeland. They may have been exposed to other religious ideas. In some way, the cultural experience of the people gave birth to the notion a mighty force beyond the world that was evil. God was still supreme. But God had significant opposition in the form of Satan.

Another example of cultural influence in the Old Testament is found in the notion of how available God is for humans. As we have noted, in the earliest stories God was an active and immediate character who conversed with people. In the later cultures of the Old Testament period, that availability began to change. God was increasingly thought of as removed and distant. As a result of the concept of an aloof God, divine intermediary agents received more attention. If God is remote, then divine agents begin to play a more significant role.

In the later Old Testament literature two primary agents function to make God accessible. Angels become more important. There is more interest in the personalities of angels and their role. Some are given names (for instance, Gabriel found in Daniel 9:21), their dress is described (for example, Daniel 10:5), and their number in the divine court increases (compare Daniel 7:9-10 and 1 Kings 22:19-23). Angels become an important communication link between the splendor of the Lord and the world.

WHAT ARE WE TO MAKE OF THE OLD TESTAMENT?

But another transmitter of God's will for the world also emerged in a later cultural period. The Hebrew people developed a concept of "wisdom." The earlier cultures dating back to the Old Testament's origins nurtured the idea that God reveals the divine will through personal appearances and speeches. But gradually the people came to appreciate the value of inherited teachings passed on through the wise elders of the community. Eventually, writers gave the wisdom of the elders a divine status. Wisdom becomes a divine person. Proverbs 8:22-31 describes Wisdom as the first of God's creation. She (*wisdom* is a feminine word in Hebrew) was with God in creation and a participant in the creative process. Consequently, through Wisdom people learn the divine will and win favor in God's eyes (Proverbs 8:32-36).

The rise of the concept of Satan, the emergence of a more prominent role for angels, and the notion of Wisdom as a female agent for God all suggest the changing cultural settings for the Old Testament literature. The Old Testament presents a variety of images of God, each connected with a cultural experience of the people. We cannot paint the entire Old Testament a single color. There are a variety of colors and there are different shades of each. Over the many years during which the Hebrew religion was born and practiced, we find experiences and ideas changing. They did not necessarily evolve for the better. They simply changed. So, the later Old Testament materials are not necessarily more valuable. Some of the earliest Old Testament ideas may be its richest (for example, Genesis 3). We turn then to the helpful messages for our lives we can find within the Old Testament.

How Can We Appreciate the Old Testament?

The Old Testament is often not appreciated among Christians. It gets painted a single color because of some of its stories and pictures of God. The truth is, however, that the first Testament of our Bible is a valuable resource for our Christian lives and faith today. Chapter 2 emphasizes the Bible's story of faith and how important that story is for our reading of Scripture. The Old Testament provides the substance of most of that story. Christ is the story's climax, but without the Old Testament the story would be incomplete. Beyond that essential contribution to our lives, the Old Testament also provides specifics that are equally important.

God's Reliable Love

"The God of the Old Testament is a God of wrath; the God of the New Testament is a God of love." You have doubtless heard this generalization. But it is wrong on both counts.

For one thing, such a generalization sweeps the wrathful portrayals of God in the New Testament under the rug. For instance, the Gospel of Matthew frequently uses the phrase "weeping and gnashing of teeth" to picture the consequences of disobedience and lack of faith (see, for example, Matthew 13:42, 50; 22:13). God is angry at the unrighteous. Second Thessalonians 1:6-10 expresses that same divine wrath. When Christ appears again in glory, angels "in flaming fire" will inflict "vengeance on those who do not know God and on those who do not obey the gospel of our Lord Jesus. These will suffer the punishment of eternal destruction, separated from the presence of the Lord. . . ."

But the generalization that the Old Testament God is a God of wrath also ignores the Old Testament's pictures of God's love. That divine love is of a particular kind. God establishes a relationship with the people of Israel through Abraham and Sarah and then again through Moses. That relationship is an agreement or covenant that God will be their God (there are many gods available) and they will be faithful in the relationship (see Genesis 12:1-3; 15:1-6; Exodus 20:1-18).

The most common word for God's love in the Old Testament has to do with God's faithfulness to this relationship. That word, *chesed,* is often translated "steadfast love" and sometimes "covenant loyalty" (for example, Deuteronomy 7:9-12). It is scattered throughout the pages of the Old Testament like diamonds. The word appears approximately 220 times in the Old Testament. It appears nearly 100 times in the book of Psalms. Read Psalm 136 where *chesed* is part of a congregational liturgical response.

The importance of this portrayal of God's love is that it is not a vague emotion of some sort, like the way we often use the word love today. *Chesed* describes a caring commitment to the people, faithfulness and loyalty to the relationship. For good reason, the Old Testament often uses the metaphor of marriage for the covenant relationship between God and the people. Hosea 1—3 is a vivid use of that analogy. The message of those chapters is that the people have been unfaithful partners in the marriage. Nonetheless, God remains faithful and accepts the adulterous spouse back (see Hosea 2:19-20).

Hosea also presents one of the most striking expressions of God's faithful love. In verses 1-9 of chapter 11, God speaks of the divine compassion for Israel. God has loved them like a parent, taught them to walk, and held them in caring arms. Yet like rebellious children, "[God's] people are bent on turning away from [God]" (verse 7). God next asks, "How can I give you up. . . ?" Then the Lord answers that question: "My heart recoils within me; my compassion grows warm and tender. I will not execute my fierce anger; . . . for I am God and no mortal, the Holy One in your midst, and I will not come in wrath" (verses 8-9).

Hosea suggests God's love is a holy and divine love, beyond the human capacity for love. The divine love is compared with that of a parent, exactly the way the New Testament characterizes God's love. Love is greater than justice. Justice alone would require that God abandon Israel and allow them to suffer the consequences of their unfaithfulness. But love has the last word. The Christian concept of Christ's crucifixion is exactly parallel. Just punishment for human sin gives way to divine love. Instead of crucifying us for our sins, God goes through death for us in Christ. Love, indeed, has the final word.

The biblical God is both just and loving. For that reason there are vivid pictures of God's anger with humans throughout the Bible. But the message of both the Testaments is that God's love prevails. God desires a committed relationship with you and me.

The Struggle with Evil

The Old Testament pictures a God of justice and love, whose loving faithfulness to the covenant with the people prevails. But it prevails in spite of human sin and unfaithfulness. This is a second specific contribution the Old Testament makes to our Christian lives and faith. Like you and me, the Hebrew people want and make a commitment to God. But their sin gets in the way of their faithfulness to that commitment. The Old Testament's portrayal of human weakness and fickleness fits us like a glove. Paul puts it in a generality: "All have sinned and fall short of the glory of God" (Romans 3:23). The Old Testament describes it in the history of a sincere and devout people.

The Hebrew people created and preserved a series of stories expressing their own experience with sin. The series in Genesis 3-11 speaks of the whole of humanity in terms of our misdirected ambitions and aspirations. Genesis 3 narrates the disobedience of Adam and Eve, who are more than individuals. They are symbols representing all of us. The succeeding stories demonstrate the brutal consequences of life alienated from God. Cain murders a brother in 4:1-16, and then Lamech murders countless others for the slightest offenses (4:23-24). Human wickedness grows so bad that God finally washes the earth clean and starts humanity afresh from a righteous few (Genesis 7:1—9:17). However strange to the modern ear these stories may sound, they capture something dreadful about us humans that we know all too well from our own experience and society.

The Old Testament also tells us something else about ourselves we already know but hesitate to admit. Human sin and brokenness are not just results of individual acts. They are social realities. The Old Testament keeps reminding us that sin has social consequences. My sin affects not just me but those around me and my children. That awful fact is put on the lips of God in Exodus 20:5: "I the Lord your God am a jealous God, punishing children for the iniquity of parents, to the third and fourth generation of those who reject me ..." That declaration is made concrete and specific in the story of David. After his sinful episode with Bathsheba and his conviction at the hands of the prophet Nathan, David repents. He is forgiven, but his child whom Bathsheba bore is put to death (2 Samuel 11:1—12:23).

Perhaps we would rather not express it in these ways. But the truth is that rejecting God has consequences for others who are close to us. Today we put that fact in rather dull language about "social conditioning." The Hebrew people did not have our understanding of social psychology. They simply attributed the social ramifications of sin to God's justice.

Israel's story is the record of the human weakness to remain faithful to our agreement with God. Time and time again the people fail to keep their end of the bargain. Repeatedly, they experience the consequences of their sinfulness. But God keeps giving them another chance. The God of the Old Testament is not just the God of the second chance but the God of fourth, fifth, and more chances.

But the Old Testament pictures another dimension of our struggle with evil. We know that "bad things happen to good people." Righteous and good people suffer unjustly. We can understand suffering as one of the consequences of sin, even the sins of others. But some of the best Christians we know are stricken with cancer or other diseases and suffer horribly before death finally relieves them. When this kind of thing happens, we feel confused.

The Old Testament depicts Israel's struggle to understand unjust suffering and death. A common teaching in part of the Old Testament simplifies the relationship between sin and suffering on the one hand, and righteousness and prosperity on the other. If you are faithful to God, you will thrive, prosper, and have a long life. If you are unfaithful, you will suffer illness, poverty, and die at an early age. Psalm 1 and Judges 2:11-23 epitomize this teaching. We often adhere to this view, sometimes unconsciously. When something unfortunate happens to you, do you ask, "What have I done to deserve this?" This overly simplistic understanding of suffering makes the reality of unjust hardship and tragedy all the more difficult to understand.

Some of the Old Testament documents tackle this question. Job is a case study in unjust suffering, or at least so he argues. His so-called friends try to get him to confess to some secret sin that has brought on all his suffering. But he stubbornly insists that he is innocent. God finally asks Job who he thinks he is to challenge the way God has made the world. "Where were you when I laid the foundation of the earth?" God asks him (Job 38:4). Job must finally simply shut up and speak no more (40:4-5). Apparently some adherent to the teaching that righteousness is always rewarded in this life added a conclusion to the book of Job. Job's fortunes are reversed, he prospers more than ever, and dies "old and full of days" (42:10-17).

The Old Testament never satisfactorily answers the question of our struggle with undeserved suffering. But it epitomizes that struggle. We can identify with its probes of the mysteries of life. Most of all we can appreciate the honesty with which Job and others struggle with the question.

Honesty before God

Job models a remarkable honesty before God. He challenges God and shakes his fist at the heavens (for example, Job 31). He is not afraid to invite a mediator to settle his dispute with God (chapter 9). Such candid address to God may take us aback. We are probably polite and reverent in our prayers. Only when tragedy strikes might we dare to question God, and, even then, we do so rather timidly. The Old Testament invites us to a personal honesty before God.

Jeremiah is another model of that candor. The book of Jeremiah is dotted with the prophet's "laments" to God. Jeremiah suffered severely as a result of his ministry. He was unpopular, ostracized, and threatened because of his message. He felt God did not treated him justly, did not aided him adequately, and even tricked him into accepting his mission. In a series of complaints before God, Jeremiah lays his feelings on the table (for instance, 11:18-20; 12:1-6; and 17:14-18). My favorite among Jeremiah's prayers of complaint is 15:10-18. There he confesses his utter discouragement and accuses God: "Truly, you are to me like a deceitful brook, like waters that fail" (15:16-18).

Jeremiah is absolutely honest with God. His prayers exemplify the kind of prayers God will hear. We cannot and do not have to hide our feelings from God. Instead, we can use prayer to get them expressed in the presence of one who understands us.

The psalms are filled with the kind of honesty before God that we witness in Job and Jeremiah (for example, Psalms 74, 79, and 137). The book of Psalms constituted Israel's hymnal and prayer book. And how honest those psalms are. Some of them go even further than Job and Jeremiah. They openly ask God to revenge the people against their enemies (for instance, 18:37-42; 94:1-7; and 149:6-9). Psalm 58, as a whole, is a prayer for vengeance. The psalmist asks God to turn the wicked "into slime" (verse 8).

What is edifying in such hateful prayers for vengeance? Surely they contradict Jesus' command that we love our enemies (Matthew 5:43-48). But how admirably honest they are! Many of us have had the feeling of hatred expressed in the psalms. I confess that I have. But are we honest enough to put that hatred before God? Can we dare to say to God what God already knows is in our hearts? The psalmists are often more honest than we are. Thereby they show us the role of prayer in dealing with negative feelings we may not like to admit, even to ourselves. The Old Testament contributes a candor to our prayer life that offers us new and perhaps seldom explored virtues of our relationship with God.

Faithfulness in the Whole of Life

One final and brief note about how the Old Testament contributes to our lives. The Old Testament's large body of laws and regulation may often turn us off. We have difficulty in understanding how, if at all, these passages have any meaning for us. The command that we "not plow with an ox and a donkey yoked together" (Deuteronomy 22:10) seems hardly relevant. But wait! Maybe there is something for us in all these commandments.

First of all, the seemingly endless regulations about the priesthood (that is, the Levites) and how proper sacrifices to God are to be offered do have a point. Granted, all the Old Testament laws regarding worship are set aside by God's act in Christ. The church has held that view for centuries. But in general they are the same kind of regulations we establish for our clergy and certain acts of worship. Seminarians are taught how to celebrate the Lord's Supper, baptize, perform a marriage, and bury the dead. The Old Testament's worship regulations constitute a "priest's manual." They provided the Hebrew people "good order" in the way in which clergy should conduct themselves and lead worship.

But far more important are the Old Testament's moral laws. Of course, they are designed for a specific culture long gone. But read the legal passages of Exodus, Leviticus, and Deuteronomy carefully and make note of all the subjects that are covered. You soon gain the impression that the laws attempt to show that obedience to God is involved in every imaginable area of life. Family life is covered (for example, Leviticus 18:13). Proper sexual activity is discussed (for example, Deuteronomy 22:22). Regulations about theft (Exodus 22:1), murder (Exodus 21:12-14), personal injury (Exodus 21:18-19), property rights (Deuteronomy 19:14), and countless other matters are made clear. Sometimes the specific occasions are described in detail. For instance, if a husband is in a fight with another man, the wife shall not grab her husband's opponent by his private parts (Deuteronomy 25:11-12)!

But the specific moral injunctions are not important here. The fact is that faithfulness to God involves the whole of our lives. There is no corner, niche, or cranny of life where God is unconcerned with how we act. The Jewish rabbis of a later time perceived this about their law and attempted to extend it even further. We Christians must agree. God's will for our lives knows no boundaries.

Of course, Old Testament law is important for many other reasons. Not least of all, it is the basis of legal systems in many parts of the world. Moreover, it demonstrates God's commitment to the needy and homeless. But for now I invite you to a new appreciation of why law and regulations are so prominent in the Old Testament.

Making Something of It

The Old Testament challenges us to make something of it. The first Testament is a formidable challenge, to be sure. It is far from easy reading. It demands that we study the history, the cultures, and the literature of this part of our canon. Reading it is not the same as the picture books of the Old Testament we used when we were children. But its promise for our lives goes unfulfilled unless we accept its challenge.

Reading the Old Testament is an exercise, too, in judging this part of the Bible by other parts. This discussion should not be misconstrued to mean we should accept uncritically everything the Old Testament has to say. We need to have a clear conception of the God of love and grace in mind as we read it. Equipped with that picture of God—found in the Old Testament itself as well as in the New Testament—we can make decisions about what is important for our lives in the documents of the first Testament.

A critical and careful reading of the Old Testament can enrich our lives in Christ. The ancient church was right, and Marcion was wrong! The Hebrew Scriptures provide an important part of a foundation for our Christian lives.

Chapter Seven ───────────
What Are They Saying about the Bible Today?

CHRISTIANS ARE NORMALLY PLEASED when the Bible gets some attention in the national press. In an increasingly pluralistic and secular society, we appreciate any publicity for Christianity. But some of what the media deems newsworthy is not always to our liking. In its usual manner, the media focuses on the sensational. And more and more in the last several decades, the news about the Bible has been of the spectacular sort: A cult group commits suicide together because the Bible teaches they will be taken to a space ship and carried off to heaven. Scholars determine Jesus did not actually say much that the Bible attributes to him. The Bible is labeled chauvinistic by feminist scholars.

Sometimes it is difficult to know what to make of such news stories. In every case, Christians wonder how representative the newsmakers are of the church and scholarship. In some cases, we puzzle over exactly how to interpret such announcements to others who are interested in Christianity and the Bible. Nearly always such announcements cause us some doubt about our own reading of Scripture. How much truth, if any, is there in such claims about the Bible? Is our interpretation sound?

What are they saying about the Bible today? We want to know and are obliged to know. Furthermore, we are responsible for determining just what to think of some sensational claims that make national headlines. There are no easy answers, and every case is complicated. An analysis of any one of the movements reported in the news is bound to be an oversimplification. So, it is worth our while to reflect on these movements. They are often significant beyond what the news media may report.

This chapter discusses only two of the movements that seem to make the news with some regularity. The discussion will try fairly to report what each movement is all about and offer an evaluation of its significance for our understanding of the Bible today.

Did Jesus Really Say That?

Many Christians have been disturbed by reports that biblical scholars are challenging the records in the four Gospels of what Jesus taught and did. In some cases, the challenge goes to the core of cherished beliefs among Christians. Did Jesus really teach the disciples the Lord's Prayer? The possibility that our faith is based on distorted representations of the real Jesus can be frightening! If we cannot trust the Gospels to inform us about Christ, what are we to believe? If scholars question the reliability of the Gospels' reports, where do we turn for a basis for faith?

Let's, first of all, try to understand what this group of scholars is up to. Then we will be in a better position to assess the value of their views.

What Is the Quest for the Historical Jesus?

The contemporary effort to describe the historical Jesus is a development of scholarship that dates back to the Enlightenment of the eighteenth century in Europe. This cultural revolution influenced biblical studies in a number of ways. Most important is the fact that the Reformation and Enlightenment gave birth to biblical criticism. In previous centuries, the church had controlled the study of the Bible, and such study was performed entirely in order to fortify the teachings of the church. The Bible was read and studied in order to provide evidence for the church's basic beliefs. The church, in effect, used the Bible for its own ends.

Critical scholarship arose, at least in part, to separate the study of the Bible from the church. All ancient literature was being studied in an analytical way. Skeptical questions were asked of it. Soon scholars began studying Scripture in the same way. They began asking if the Bible were true. Did it accurately report historical events? Of course, these questions were asked and answered in terms of what the scholarly culture of the time believed was true. The authority of reason replaced the church's authority. In a sense, one set of dogmatic beliefs succeeded another. Instead of reading the Bible from the perspective of the church's beliefs, many read it in the light of what was assumed to be culturally true. For the most part, critical scholarship assumed reason and scientific truth could determine what was true.

Over the centuries, fortunately, critical scholarship has matured a good deal since its childhood. It has asked critical questions of its own way of studying the Bible. Moreover, it has produced an enormous number of valuable insights into the Bible. Those insights have greatly enriched our understanding of Scripture. Not least of all, it has shed considerable light on the four Gospels of our New Testament.

The Gospels' reports of Jesus interested critical scholarship. The effort to construct a historically accurate picture of Jesus evolved out of that interest for several reasons. The first is the recognition that the Gospels themselves are at least equally as devoted to preaching a faith in Jesus as they are to reporting the historical facts about him. So the quest for the historical Jesus attempted to separate faith and fact in the Gospels.

The second reason scholars began seeking the historical Jesus is that they believed there was a purely factual Jesus to be found. One's faith should be based, they argued, on the actual events of history rather than on the early Christians' faith in Jesus. Hence, their efforts entailed stripping away the early faith in Christ in order to discover the "real Jesus."

Today, when we read the "lives of Jesus" written in the nineteenth century, we see clearly that the authors found the Jesus they wanted to find. Their own cultural values are clear in what they choose to regard as historical facts. For that reason, among others, the quest for the historical Jesus faded away into sunset. More recent scholars were skeptical of the methods their predecessors used to define what was historical. Around the middle of the twentieth century, however, the quest for the historical Jesus surfaced again in what has sometimes been called the "new quest." It tried to find a basis in the Gospels' representation of Jesus on which to determine who Jesus actually was and what he really taught. But it too went the way of the first quest, rejected, in part, because, once again, these scholars' read their own values into the biblical stories.

The now notorious "Jesus Seminar" group developed what some are calling the "third quest." A group of very learned and

esteemed biblical interpreters again undertook the task of sepa-
rating fact and faith. The difference is that these contemporary
scholars work as a team. They study a particular text in one of
the Gospels. Then they take a vote on what is historically accurate in the passage. The criteria vary for determining whether or
not something is historical. Each scholar brings his or her own
view of what might have originated with Jesus and what might
have been added by the early church. Some, for instance, believe
that any saying or action attributed to Jesus that parallels some
teaching or action cherished in the early church cannot be original with Jesus. To facilitate their voting, they created a number
of categories for classification. On the one extreme are those features of a passage that are clearly not historical. On the other end
are those that are certainly historical. In between are two other
categories that label something as "possibly historical" or "likely
un-historical."

Actually, much of the scholarly work of the Jesus Seminar is
not unusual. It is the seminar's practice of coming to a democra-
tic judgment about a passage that is unique among scholarly
biblical groups today. The group published its conclusions in
The Five Gospels: The Search for the Authentic Words of Jesus
(HarperCollins Publishers, 1996). The fifth gospel is the Gospel
of Thomas, written sometime in the second century. Some
believe it preserves authentic sayings of Jesus. In their publication, the Jesus Seminar claims that no more than 20 percent of
the sayings attributed to Jesus were actually spoken by him. The
text of *The Five Gospels* is printed in the four different colors,
representing the various categories of judgment regarding the
historical accuracy of parts of each passage. Red represents the
historically true portions of each Gospel. Their "red-lettered edition of the Bible" earned the group some notoriety. Perhaps it is
no accident that this red-letter edition is very different from
those sold in most Bible book stores! Some of the leading figures
in the movement have also undertaken to write reconstructions
of the historical Jesus. These too have attracted the news media
and stirred considerable controversy.

The Jesus Seminar and its leaders are courageous. Gradually
the leaders of the group have made it clear that they hope to

impact contemporary Christian belief. In 1996 the seminar's founder and leader, Robert W. Funk, published a book entitled, *Honest to Jesus: Jesus for a New Millennium* (San Francisco: HarperSanFrancisco, 1996). In this book, Funk makes clear that he hopes his new picture of the historical Jesus will cultivate a fresh spirituality, one that he believes is more appropriate for the twenty-first century than traditional Christian faith. For Funk the destruction of the popular image of Jesus and a literalist reading of the Gospels is necessary in order that we can perceive more truthfully what Jesus was attempting to accomplish in his lifetime.

What Is Valuable about this Movement?

I was a member of the Jesus Seminar for several years during its early years. Many of my colleagues in New Testament study gathered for the meetings to share their insights into selected Gospel passages. I appreciated the discussions and the stimulation I gained from my participation. But, frankly, I thought "voting" on the historical value of features of a passage was rather silly. Moreover, I was concerned that the seminar's leaders seemed to delight in the news media's publication of the more sensational conclusions the group came to at their meetings. After about two years, I quietly allowed my membership to lapse.

A number of observations about this movement will help assess its value for our understanding of the Bible.

We read the Bible through cultural glasses. All efforts to discover the Jesus of history in the Gospels betray the seekers' own values. In this way, the newest quest for the historical Jesus is no different from earlier quests. The Jesus they find hidden away in the Gospels is a Jesus constructed in terms of late-twentieth-century North American cultural values.

Not accidentally, the historical Jesus this movement finds is generally a Jesus who was committed to radical social change and liberation from oppression. At the close of the twentieth century, our society has increasingly recognized those values as important and necessary for us. Moreover, it is true, I believe, that the Jesus of the Gospels did share those concerns. What the

Jesus Seminar movement has done, however, is strip Jesus of all other concerns and commitments.

These scholars demonstrate the inescapable fact that we read Scripture out of our own cultural context. The values that we embrace by virtue of our cultural conditioning are like glasses through which we see the world and, in this case, the biblical message. But precisely because this fact is so evident, we ought to beware of it. When we recognize that our cultural glasses make us see certain things more clearly than others, we can broaden our vision and try to look more carefully for the other messages in the Bible.

One of the Bible's roles in contemporary life is to challenge what we take for granted. For example, many efforts to paint a picture of Jesus as he actually was eliminate all his teachings having to do with God's final act to redeem the world. Matthew 24:29-51 does not compute in the modern mind. We do not think in terms of God finally intervening to remake our world. Unless we destroy ourselves, we assume the course of human events will go on interminably. But Jesus' message about the appearance of "the Son of Man in heaven" may be one we need to hear—as disruptive as it may be. The Bible's "eschatology" (that is, teachings about "last things") suggests that history has a divine goal, purpose, and intention. In the twentieth century we have experienced a period of history that does not make much sense. Maybe the Bible forces us to think about God's goal for history.

We cannot take off our cultural glasses. But we can squint through them to see something we may not want to see and then take that seriously.

History is not pure facts. The Jesus Seminar and others who want to find the historical Jesus assume that the figure portrayed in the Gospels is inadequate. They believe that faith should be grounded on pure and unadulterated historical fact. They are not alone in that belief. Some conservative Christians argue that the Bible reports pure history, and that history is grounds for faith. The Gospels of Matthew and Luke (but not Mark and John) both teach that Jesus was born of a virgin. This is a historical fact some

Christians argue. Because it is fact they continue, we can be sure of our faith.

All such efforts to distinguish between historical fact and the interpretation of facts are dangerous. History is not pure fact. It is always someone's or some community's interpretation of the facts. Just listen to the varying reports of an auto accident, and you quickly see that facts are all mixed up in perception. Perception, as psychology has taught us, is selective. We see only portions—usually only the portions we want to see—of all there is to see. History is not the simple recitation of all the events of a particular period of time. History always entails decisions about which are the important events, what caused them, and what their consequences are.

Strangely enough, the radical scholars who challenge the Gospels' accounts of Jesus embrace a similar view of history much like the one held by conservative Christians. But these Christians think the radical scholars are Satan's instruments. Both their understandings of history are overly simple. History always entails interpretation from perspective. The Gospel writers clearly interpret the historical fact of Jesus' life differently than did the Romans of the same period. The Gospels boldly claim that in the historical Jesus they see one who was God's only child and the agent of divine salvation. The Gospels are proclamations of Jesus and not simply reports of facts about his life and ministry. But so, too, is the new memorial to Franklin D. Roosevelt in Washington, D.C. It proclaims FDR's importance to America even as it also reports selected events in his presidency.

The New Testament Jesus is all we need. We do not read the Gospels for a simple factual report of Jesus' ministry. We read them to learn what the first Christians believed about him. To be sure, that reading includes some historical facts. But the important thing for us is what the Gospels claim about those facts. They are events in which God was at work for the benefit of humanity.

You and I do not need to separate fact from interpretation. It is the combination of the two that really matters to us. The question of whether or not the early Christians correctly interpreted

Jesus is the important thing. To be a Christian today entails sharing the faith of our first ancestors. Perhaps we need not share every detail of their faith perception of Jesus. Some of those details are not relevant for us. But we do need to share a faith in the substance of their claim that in Christ God was doing something new to create a relationship of love with us.

In the final analysis, all we need are the stories of Jesus in the Gospels and the faith of the early Christians in him found elsewhere in the New Testament. We do not need a video or audio recording of Jesus' acts and teachings. Even if we had those factual recordings, we would still have to decide how we were going to interpret them. The Gospels, along with the grace of God, are all we need to put our faith in what the first Christians believed God was doing through Jesus.

The scholars' quest to separate historical facts about Jesus from the faith story of the Gospels may be an interesting endeavor. It also is fraught with difficulties. But their findings make us think. Certainly the proposal that Jesus offered an oppressed people new hope is a valuable contribution, even if we believe Jesus did far more. Yet, the relevance of the Bible for our lives is in no way dependent on these particular scholarly efforts.

Does the Bible Teach Male Chauvinism?

A different kind of challenge comes from another group of scholars. In recent years, an increasing number of interpreters have asked us to consider whether the Bible depicts women as inferior to men and perpetuates a view of women's subservience to men's authority. These scholars have influenced a good many laity, and the movement's charge that the Bible is chauvinistic is broader than the scholarly community. Again let's summarize this movement before evaluating its importance for the church's reading and interpretation of Scripture.

The Woman's Bible
The women's movement, especially in the United States, has had a considerable effect on the church. Among other things, many Christian men, as well as women, have rethought the relationship

between the sexes. Women, once limited to service mainly in church kitchens, function as equals in the life of the church. They now hold offices once reserved exclusively for men, both in local congregations and in the wider institutions of the church. A number of the major church bodies now ordain women for ministry. In some cases, enrollment of women in seminaries outnumbers male enrollment.

Female biblical scholars have also risen to prominence. They are respected colleagues and leaders in the professional organizations of those who teach biblical studies in colleges, universities, and seminaries. Many of them have been at the forefront of a movement to view the Bible through the eyes of women. At the level of scholarship, many males have joined forces with them in this endeavor. Now what is called a "feminist" reading of Scripture is a widespread and productive enterprise comprised of both men and women.

The movement has yielded rich results. First, many now recognize that men were primarily responsible for the writing of the biblical documents. Men have also traditionally been the interpreters of Scripture in the church. The Bible and its interpretation has been dominated by the male perspective. The recognition of this truth impacts the Bible's interpretation in significant ways. Male scholars, for instance, are now sensitive to the traditional masculine readings of passages and of the masculine perspective that dominates the contents of Scripture.

Second, the women's movement has energized a new interest in the way the Bible portrays female characters. On the one hand, there is a new appreciation for the role women play in the Bible's story of faith. As a result, characters such as Deborah, Ruth, Mary, Mary Magdalene, and others are seen as models of faith. For instance, the book of Judges portrays Deborah as stronger than her male colleague, Barak. When called to do battle with the enemy, Barak says to Deborah, "If you will go with me, I will go; but if you will not go with me, I will not go" (Judges 4:8). On the basis of John 20:1-18, one male Roman Catholic scholar calls Mary Magdalene "the apostle to the apostles." She is the first to whom the risen Christ appears, and she shares the news of the resurrection with the other disciples.

On the other hand, we also recognize how female characters are often portrayed as minor contributors to the biblical drama. How many women, for instance, in the Gospel stories remain unnamed? Think, for instance, of the widow of Nain in Luke 7:11-17 or the poor widow in Luke 21:1-4. The text of Mark 5:24b-34 never quotes the speech of the woman whom Jesus heals, except when she speaks to herself. In Genesis 2, woman is created out of man to provide him with a partner. Genesis 3 portrays Eve as the one who first succumbs to the temptation to disobey God and leads Adam to follow suit. Her punishment for disobedience is in her biological function as the bearer of children (3:16). In many cases, women are not portrayed in a very positive light in biblical stories.

Still a third contribution the feminist movement has made is in how scholars have begun to study certain biblical passages in a new light. In Romans 16:1-16 Paul concludes his letter with personal greetings to some of the leaders of the church in Rome. Phoebe is first on the list. She is called a "deacon" of a congregation and a "benefactor" of many, among whom Paul includes himself. No less than nine other women are included in the list of those to whom Paul sends his greetings. Through the study of passages such as this, scholars have gained a new understanding of the role women played in the earliest Christian churches. Before the influence of feminist scholars, I regularly skimmed that passage as relatively unimportant.

Exodus 15:21 is another example of the impact the feminist movement has had on biblical studies. Miriam's song of praise for God's deliverance indicates her leadership in the Israelites liberation from their bondage as slaves. The preservation of these stories about the exodus tended to highlight Moses. But the presence of Miriam's song demonstrates his sister's significance. She interprets the meaning of Israel's escape and thus assumes the function of a prophet. Moreover, Miriam suggests that women originated more of Israel's poetic songs than has usually been recognized in the past. Were some of the psalms originally written by women?

Indeed, a fourth result of the insights of this movement challenges our easy judgment that the biblical authors were exclusively male. There is little doubt that in the Bible's patriarchal cultures men were responsible for writing. But Paul himself used a secretary since he wrote so poorly (read Galatians 6:11). Perhaps some biblical documents are actually the work of women. In some cases, there is little reason to dismiss that prospect. Some have argued in particular that the Gospel of John and Hebrews could possibly be the work of Christian women.

Of course, these are questions that can never be settled. Moreover, the reasons for determining the gender of an author are at best questionable. The perspective of the author, the contents of the book, and the way in which women are treated within a document are not firm bases for deciding whether or not the author was male or female. But the challenge not to dismiss the possibility of female authorship makes us rethink Scripture.

These four contributions of the feminist interpretation to biblical studies are only suggestive of the impact the movement has had on our contemporary reading of the Bible. Female scholars have also stimulated biblical research on violence and warfare, the family, and the language used of God. The movement they have led has now become widely influential in biblical interpretation.

Female biblical scholars mark the work of Elizabeth Cady Stanton and the publication of *The Woman's Bible* in the 1890s as the beginning of the movement in North America. To celebrate the one-hundredth anniversary of that publication, some of them collaborated on *The Woman's Bible Commentary*. The book is a good introduction to the concerns of the movement as a whole. (See Suggestions for Further Reading.)

An extreme wing of the feminist movement, however, disavows the Bible entirely. Because they believe the Bible is so thoroughly chauvinistic in its perspective, they regard it beyond redemption. According to them, the Bible oppresses women, justifying female subservience to male authority. Some have even abandoned their Christian faith as a whole because of what they experience as the hopelessly patriarchal character of the church and its fundamental beliefs. That extreme minority is, however, not representative of the entire feminist movement. The vast majority of feminist interpreters are committed to furthering a more inclusive interpretation of Scripture. In effect they hope to free the Bible of its chauvinism toward women both in terms of its content and its interpretation.

The challenge of the movement as a whole may be summarized in two assertions: First, the Bible, for the most part, was written by men out of the context of a patriarchal culture and is thus chauvinistic in its treatment of women. Second, the Bible's interpretation was controlled by men throughout the church's life.

What Is Valuable about This Movement?

In response to both challenges issuing from the movement, the only honest answer must be: "Right on both counts."

The Bible's male chauvinism. Earlier sections of this book have already noted the Bible's tendency to minimize women and their roles. The documents of the Bible were written out of various cultures over a period of two thousand years. But each of those cultures was, indeed, patriarchal. The precise role of women, however, varied somewhat in each of them.

The male dominance of the origin of the Bible is part of the way in which it expresses a cultural setting. It is like the understanding of the world and space in Scripture. Both Testaments assume a flat world. God is above the world in the heavens. In some mysterious place below the world is the realm of the dead (*sheol* in the Old Testament and hell or hades in the New Testament). One goes up to reach God. Consequently, Christ descended to this world from his heavenly home (John 3:13) and after his resurrection, ascends to return to God (for example, Luke 24:51). The "up" and "down" of the biblical view of the world are expressions of cultural understandings of the time. Today up and down are understood differently. They are functions of our planet's gravity and, once beyond that force, up and down have little meaning.

The biblical assumption that men are superior to women is similar. It is part of the cultural setting out of which and for which the Bible was written. Colossians 3:18-24 provides us a thumbnail sketch of the structure of the family in the period during which the New Testament was written. The husband was the "lord" of the family. All the family members were subjects of his rule. Wives were second in the hierarchy, followed by children, and below them slaves. The leaders of the first church nurtured that pattern among Christian families. In Acts we hear of the baptism of entire households (for example, Acts 18:8). When the husband was baptized, so too were his wife, children, and slaves.

Even more important, the feminist movement in biblical interpretation questions Scripture's prevalent use of masculine images for God. Because men were "little lords" in the cultures of both the Testaments, God is continually pictured with male language. King, Lord, Husband, Warrior, and especially Father are all masculine names used to represent God. However, feminist interpreters (including many who are men) draw our attention to passages in which God is pictured in feminine language. God is compared to a comforting mother in Isaiah 66:13, Ezekiel 19:2-9, and Psalm 131:2 ("like a weaned child with its mother"). Jesus speaks of his desire to embrace Jerusalem like a mother hen protects her chicks under her wing (Matthew 23:37 and Luke 13:34). Interestingly, these images of God express the divine care, comfort, and nurture we all know and value so highly.

Because the biblical documents arose out of patriarchal cultures, they speak most often of God in masculine terms. The movement afoot today invites us also to appreciate the value of feminine names and metaphors for God in the Bible. It asks us to recognize that Scripture does sometimes attribute feminine characteristics to God. God is both father and mother to us—a heavenly parent who offers us the gifts of both the ideal mother and father. With a wider range of words to speak of God, we find we are better able to say what we experience in divine love and care.

Hence, the feminist interpretation sensitizes us to the difference between our culture and the biblical cultures. It challenges us to separate teachings that perpetuate the dominance of men from the Bible's central message. These scholars denounce the demeaning of women in the Bible. They dare us to see the biblical God as one who calls all humans as instruments of the divine will.

Feminine interpreters sometimes speak of the Bible as containing "prototypes" for our lives. A prototype is a first model. It is not necessarily the model from which the final product will be produced. Improvements, adaptations, and adjustments will be made in the final product. The biblical pictures of the way our new relationship with God issues in moral living are prototypes for us, not exact models. These first drafts of moral life are often patriarchal because they were conceived for life in cultures that were constructed on the assumption of male superiority. But we can adjust the prototypes for life in a more inclusive culture in which men and women are equals.

The chauvinism of biblical interpretation. The patriarchy of the Bible has been perpetuated by its interpretation through the nearly two thousand years of church history. Men have traditionally been the church's leaders and clergy. Scholars, moreover, were ordinarily men with very few exceptions. They interpreted the Bible for others. The second charge leveled by the feminist movement, then, is also true.

In the past, interpreters have been negligent in considering women's experience. They have glided past passages that provide important hints about the role of women in God's plan of salvation. They have ignored the feminine language the Bible sometimes uses for God. All in all, with some notable exceptions, biblical interpreters in the past have tended to protect their own social positions of authority and power.

Male biblical interpreters prior to the late twentieth century, for example, are responsible in large part for a number of misguided popular views of some biblical women. Curiously, they have (perhaps unintentionally) created the notion that Mary Magdalene had been a prostitute. In fact, the portrayal of her in the Gospels supplies no evidence for that impression. Luke tells us that she was among a group of women who followed Jesus and that she had been freed of "seven demons" (Luke 8:1-3). In the Gospel of John she was one of Jesus' disciples who remained with him through his crucifixion (John 19:25-27), the first to go to Jesus' tomb, and the first to see the risen Christ (John 20:1-18).

Past interpreters have also tended to portray other biblical women as unseemly characters. All four Gospels tell a story of a woman who anoints Jesus and whose deed Jesus then defends and praises (Matthew 26:6-13 and Mark 14:3-9). In the Gospel of John that woman is Mary of Bethany, sister of Lazarus (John 12:1-8). But the Gospel of Luke (7:36-50) gives the story a slightly different twist. There she is called "a sinner." Like Matthew and Mark, Luke speaks frequently of Jesus' association with sinners (for example, Luke 15:2). It is a label that describes one who has violated any of the religious regulations of the time. But interpreters have tended to identify this particular woman's sin as sexual. She is often described as a prostitute. In a similar way, these interpreters quickly condemn the Samaritan woman who meets Jesus at the well (John 4:1-42) for her sexual behavior. Jesus, however, never condemns her!

Male interpreters have often protected the authority of men that the Bible seems to authorize. The feminist interpretation movement challenges this tradition and invites us to rethink some of what we have come to think of as true about the Bible. This is not to condemn all biblical interpretation before the beginning of the feminist interpretation movement. It is simply to recognize a certain nearsightedness that afflicted many earlier scholars and to correct such myopia. This is possible now, thanks to the efforts of feminist interpreters of the Bible.

Conclusions. The scholars who form the woman's movement in biblical studies have done us a great service. They have opened our eyes to an unpleasant truth about the Bible, and they have shown us a weakness of some of its interpretations. They have freed Scripture of its own cultural bonds and of one kind of faulty interpretation.

Unfortunately, the movement is sometimes accused of trying to destroy our faith in Scripture and its use in the church. The opposite is true of the feminine interpreters who I know personally and those whose works I read. Because they love the church and Scripture, they labor to allow the Bible to speak its liberating message among us. Many are convinced that, when freed to do so, Scripture will open new and exciting vistas for our lives together.

The feminist interpretation movement invites us to new appreciation of what our Bible is and how it can be interpreted. I suggest we accept the invitation.

What Are We Saying about the Bible Today?

Today, two significant movements challenge us. The quest for the historical Jesus in the Gospels invites us to consider the relation between historical fact and its interpretation. The feminist interpreters ask us to recognize the patriarchal dimension of Scripture and its past reading. These two put us on the speaker's platform. What are we going to say?

Many voices in our contemporary society appeal to Scripture. Some of those voices are shrill and harsh. The Bible, some say, predicts the end of the world in the new millennium, while others claim it has nothing to say about such an event. Some argue that it condemns homosexuality and others that it embraces gays and lesbians as God's children. So many voices. So many messages.

In all the noise, the voices of the common Christian laity may be silenced. The Bible is the people's book. It belongs to the people of God, the church. Martin Luther believed this so deeply that he translated the Bible into the German language so the German people could read it for themselves and claim it as their own.

Today, there are new reasons for Christians to reclaim the Bible. We may feel intimidated by certain Christian sisters and brothers who know the Bible better than we do. We may feel bullied by the scholars whose knowledge exceeds our own. But the time has come for Christian laity to say, "It's my Bible, too!" It is time for the laity to teach the scholars something about Scripture and how it speaks to us today. It is time to take possession of the book that is our source of life and love, and of peace and joy. It is time to open the Bible.

What are *we* going to say about the Bible?

Suggestions for Further Reading

The following are some books you may find helpful in understanding the Bible, its role in the church, and its interpretation. A brief comment about each attempts to explain why it is in this list.

The HarperCollins Study Bible, New Revised Standard Version With the Apocryphal/Deuterocanonical Books. Wayne A. Meeks, general editor. New York: HarperCollins Publishers, 1993. The articles and annotations are by members of the Society of Biblical Literature and include material from some of the finest biblical scholars.

HarperCollins Bible Dictionary. Revised Edition. Paul J. Achtemeier, general editor. New York: HarperCollins Publishers, 1996. This is the best one-volume dictionary of biblical terms and names. Contributors are selected members of the Society of Biblical Literature.

HarperCollins Bible Commentary. James L. Mays, general editor. New York: HarperCollins Publishers, 1988. The best one-volume commentary on the Bible intended for the laity. Once again, the Society of Biblical Literature provided the excellent contributors.

The New Interpreter's Bible: A Commentary in Twelve Volumes. Leander E. Keck, chair of the editorial board. Nashville: Abingdon Press, 1997–. This series is still being published. Among the volumes currently available, volume one has a number of helpful articles on the whole Bible and the Old Testament, and volume eight contains articles on the New Testament. The writers are all esteemed and gifted. The commentary on each biblical book includes "reflections" on the relationship of the message of the text and our lives today.

The Anchor Bible Dictionary. David Noel Freedman, editor-in-chief. New York: Doubleday, 1992. Six volumes. This is the most recent and comprehensive Bible dictionary available in English. It is sometimes very technical but is a treasure-house of information on a wide variety of biblical subjects.

The Beginners' Guide Series. Minneapolis: Augsburg Publishers, 1991. Several of the volumes in this series are intended to guide laity in a pursuit of biblical knowledge. *A Beginner's Guide to Reading the Bible,* by Craig Koester, provides an overview of the contents of the Bible and the Bible's formation. *A Beginner's Guide to Studying the Bible,* by Rolf E. Aaseng, presents differing ways of studying Scripture and using study helps. *A Beginner's Guide to the Books of the Bible,* by Diane L. Jacobson and Robert Kysar, gives a brief summary of and introduction to each of the books of the Bible.

Westminster Bible Companion. Patrick D. Miller and David L. Bartlett, series editors. Louisville: Westminster John Knox Press, 1995–. Each volume in this series is devoted to one or more biblical books and designed to assist laity in meaningful Bible study. The authors are well-known scholar-teachers and good communicators.

Reading the Bible Book by Book: An Introductory Study Guide to the Separate Books of the Bible with Apocrypha. By Richard Hiers. Minneapolis: Augsburg Fortress, 1988. This volume provides a thorough treatment of each book, its historical setting and importance for contemporary life, including the deuterocanonical literature.

The Book of God: The Bible as a Novel. By Walter Wangerin Jr. Grand Rapids: Zondervan Publishers, 1996. The author is a master storyteller and in this volume retells thirty-nine stories of characters and themes in an engaging way. A good introduction to the contents of the Bible.

The Real Jesus: The Misguided Quest for the Historical Jesus and the Truth of the Traditional Gospels. By Luke Timothy Johnson. New York: HarperCollins Publishers, 1996. This is the best and most thorough critique of the efforts of the Jesus Seminar written by an established New Testament scholar and a colorful writer.

The Women's Bible Commentary. Carol A. Newsom and Sharon H. Ringe, editors. Louisville: Westminster John Knox Press and SPCK, 1992. A group of female scholars provide brief commentaries on the biblical books with special attention to women and their lives as well as some general articles on women in the Bible. A good introduction to feminist interpretation of the Bible.

Questions for ——— Reflection and Discussion

Introduction: What's Become of the Bible?
1. As you begin your reading of this book, what are some of the most pressing questions you have about the Bible?
2. What sort of change in the interpretation of the Bible have you experienced, and how did you feel about it?

Chapter 1. How Do I Know What Is True?
1. What are the strengths and weakness of each of the five tests of truth explored in this chapter—experience, culture, reason, tradition, and the Bible?
2. Which of the five do you depend on most? Does this vary depending on the area of your life you are considering?
3. What do you believe we can know with certainty?

Chapter 2. What Can We Expect of the Bible?
1. What was your experience of the Bible when you were a child and a young adult? What has your experience of the Bible been in your life since?
2. In no more than a dozen words, complete this sentence: "The Bible is . . ."
3. In what sense is the Bible an authority in your life?

Chapter 3. Why So Many Different Interpretations?
1. What is the most vivid example of the differences in the interpretation of Bible you know?
2. The chapter compares two views: that the Bible has authority within itself, and that we ourselves give the Bible its authority. What are the strengths and weakness of each view? Which do you favor? Why?
3. How does each of these views influence how we approach the Bible? (continued on next page)

Chapter 3. Why So Many Different Interpretations? (cont.)
4. How do you understand the Bible to be inspired?
5. What does it mean for you to say that the Bible is the word of God?

Chapter 4. Is Something Lost in Translation?
1. What did you find most interesting or helpful in the section "How Did We Get the Bible?" How does this knowledge affect your attitude toward the Bible?
2. What did you find most disturbing in this chapter?
3. Which translations of the Bible have you used? Which do you prefer? Why?

Chapter 5. How Can I Find Meaning in the Bible?
1. Use the Bible study process outlined in this chapter to study one of these texts:
    Genesis 15:1-6; Psalm 8; Amos 5:18-34; Matthew 22:15-22; and 1 Corinthians 1:10-17.
    How well did the process work for you?
2. In the course of describing the process of Bible study, the author spoke of his own experience of finding meaning for his life in Mark 5:24b-34. Have you ever had a similar experience? What was it?

Chapter 6. What Are We to Make of the Old Testament?
1. What has been your experience in reading the Old Testament or hearing it read?
2. Which of the ideas in this chapter did you find to be most helpful?
3. Which of the themes in the section "How Can We Appreciate the Old Testament?" speak most directly to your heart and mind?

Chapter 7. What Are They Saying about the Bible Today?
1. What information about the Bible have you seen or heard in the media. How have they influenced your attitudes toward the Bible? (continued on next page)

Chapter 7. What Are They Saying about the Bible Today? (cont.)

2. If we cannot trust the Gospels to inform us about Christ, what are we to believe?

3. How do you respond to the issues raised by feminist readers of the Bible?

4. Summarize what this book tries to teach by responding to the three statements in the subtitle of the book: What the Bible is. Where it came from. What it means.

5. What in this book have you found most helpful to your understanding of the Bible? What is most disturbing? What questions do you still have? What might be your next step in "opening the Bible"?

Printed in the United States
23505LVS00002B/109-810

9 780806 635941